UNFINISHED STORIES
FOR FACILITATING DECISION MAKING IN THE ELEMENTARY CLASSROOM

Elizabeth Hirzler Weiner, Editor

nea
National Education Association
Washington, D.C.

Copyright © 1980
National Education Association of the United States

372.62
Un 2
127706
Feb-1984

Note
This collection features some revised Unfinished Stories from the series which first appeared in Today's Education: NEA Journal. Reprinted by permission.

The Editor
Elizabeth Hirzler Weiner was formerly a teacher in the Greenwich, Connecticut, public schools; she is currently an educational researcher and writer. Ms. Weiner is the editor of two other NEA publications: Sex Role Stereotyping in the Schools, second revised edition, and Discipline in the Classroom.

Library of Congress Cataloging in Publication Data
Main entry under title:

Unfinished stories for facilitating decision making in the elementary classroom.

  (Analysis and action series)
  1. Decision-making — Study and teaching (Elementary) 2. Readers (Elementary) 3. Decision-making — Juvenile literature. I. Weiner, Elizabeth Hirzler. II. Series.
LB1062.5.U53   372.6'2   79-26019
ISBN 0-8106-1678-5

Contents

Forward: How To Use These Stories 5

Responsibility and Commitment to Oneself and Others

What Should Rebecca Do?/*Assertiveness* 7
What Should Joshua Do?/*Assertiveness* 8
What Should Gail Do?/*Belonging* 9
What Should Armando Do?/*Conflict* 11
What Should Kelly Do?/*Conflict* 12
What Should Andy Do?/*Honesty* 14
What Should Emily Do?/*Kindness* 15
What Should Jonathan Do?/*Kindness* 16
What Should the Class Do?/*Kindness* 17
What Should George Do?/*Responsibility* 18
What Should Frank Do?/*Responsibility* 20
What Should Pete Do?/*Rumor* 21
What Should Norman Do?/*Rumor* 22
What Should Gloria Do?/*Self-Control* 23
What Should Peggy Do?/*Telling* 24
What Should Carol Do?/*Telling* 26
What Should Tyrone Do?/*Telling* 27

Personal Shortcomings

What Should Susie Do?/*Anger* 29
What Should Benny Do?/*Anger* 30
What Should Gwendolyn Do?/*Assertiveness* 31
What Should Bruce do?/*Assertiveness* 33
What Should Larry Do?/*Assertiveness* 34
What Should Bernard Do?/*Assertiveness* 35
What Should Guy Do?/*Assertiveness* 36
What Should Gerri Do?/*Assertiveness* 38
What Should Samantha Do?/*Cheating* 39
What Should Donald Do?/*Conflict* 40
What Should Michael Do?/*Disappointment* 41
What Should Ramona Do?/*Honesty* 43
What Should Thomas do?/*Honesty* 44

What Should Anne Do?/*Lying* 45
What Should Marcie do?/*Pride* 47
What Should Donna Do?/*Privacy* 48
What Should Jimmy Do?/*Rebellion* 49
What Should Clyde Do?/*Self-Control* 50
What Should Stephanie Do?/*Stealing* 51
What Should Maria Do?/*Stealing* 53
What Should Nicolas Do?/*Telling* 54

Shortcomings of Others
What Should Lanie Do?/*Assertiveness* 56
What Should Doug do?/*Assertiveness* 57
What Should Molly Do?/*Assertiveness* 58
What Should Bill Do?/*Assertiveness* 59
What Should Lisa and Nancy Do?/*Avoidance (fights)* 60
What Should Ray Do?/*Bragging* 61
What Should Gabrielle Do?/*Cheating* 63
What Should Scott's Class Do?/*Discrimination* 64
What Should Moira Do?/*Fairness* 66
What Should Alan Do?/*Friendship (boy-girl)* 67
What Should Sherry Do?/*Help* 68
What Should Cicely Do?/*Identity* 69
What Should Glen Do?/*Identity* 70
What Should Jacob Do?/*Identity* 72
What Should David Do?/*Loyalty* 73
What Should Kevin Do?/*Responsibility* 74
What Should Marlene Do?/*Shoplifting* 76
What Should Irene Do?/*Unhappiness* 77

FORWARD: HOW TO USE THESE STORIES

This new collection of *Unfinished Stories* can be used in a wide variety of ways to aid your students in the complex process of decision making. Designed for use in the elementary classroom, *Unfinished Stories* reflects many of the real problems, situations, and questions youngsters at this age level experience, grapple with, and must respond to daily.

How the story ends, and why, is the obvious creative writing assignment. Another might be to ask students to state concisely the possible decisions and/or assess the values found in the story. Dramatizations and story illustrations are also effective. Improvisational solutions reached by different teams of role-playing students can be exciting, particularly when the story selected is similar to a current situation in your school or classroom. And through open discussions, students can probe the depth and complexity of the important issues raised in this volume.

The stories are divided into three broad categories—Responsibility and Commitment to Oneself and Others, Personal Shortcomings, and Shortcomings of Others. A single word in the table of contents pinpoints the main, although not only, concept found in the story, and each is preceded by a brief descriptive paragraph and concludes with suggested topics for discussion.

After deciding what form student involvement and response will take, the teacher must be careful not to impose his/her own opinions or judgments. It is important that the *students* determine if Andy is stealing or "only getting what's owed" him if he keeps the extra change the cashier mistakenly gave him, how Gwen can learn to speak up for herself, or whether Alan and Zoe have a reasonable chance, and a right, to be friends without being teased by their peers.

The selected story may be read to the class by the teacher, a student or several students, or it may be duplicated for individual and small-group use. (Please observe the copyright law when duplicating by giving credit to the NEA.)

Teachers might consider having students use tape recorders as an aid in developing reading skills or to record their group's discussion for sharing with the entire class. Inviting outside people into the classroom can open new avenues for presentation or discussion: the drama teacher, for example, to assist your students in dramatizing a story; the coach to lead a discussion about fairness ("What Should Moira Do?"); the counselor, or an expert from the community, to delve into issues of race relations ("What Should Scott's Class Do?"); a member of the police department to explore ways of coping with harassment going to and from school ("What Should Doug Do?"); or a parent might participate in a discussion about burdening family responsibilities ("What Should Sherry Do?"), and so on.

Whatever form is used, teachers will find it valuable for students to explore the options the story presents, fix the point at which, and how, the course of events might have been altered, probe the moral and ethical values they discover, and determine the practical implications of such values on their lives—as individuals and as members of a particular school community.

Elizabeth Hirzler Weiner, Editor

WHAT SHOULD REBECCA DO?

Rebecca loved to write, but reading aloud was very difficult for her. Now the teacher had asked her to write the class play and she was terrified she would be expected to act in it.

Sometimes she thought she would run away. Sometimes she thought she would be sick. Sometimes she thought she would just stand up there in front of the room and yell until somebody made her sit down.

The problem was that Rebecca liked to write stories, but she hated to stand up and read them aloud. She would rather have been buried alive under a person-eating ant hill than stand up and read one of her stories. David and Sarah, her older brother and sister, had never felt that way about what they wrote. Sarah would rather get to read what she had written to the class than eat a chocolate sundae, and David was almost that bad.

Miss Endicott had taught both David and Sarah. The first day Rebecca arrived she said, "Well, well, another Kramer!" And then she told the whole class what good writers the older Kramer children were, and said, "I know we'll all enjoy hearing what Rebecca writes this year."

This was nothing new. Her last two teachers had made her read her compositions aloud, thinking they were giving her a big treat, and every year she hated it more.

Her problem was coming to a head, now. The sixth grade put on a play each year, and this year, Miss Endicott had asked Rebecca to write one. She was dying to. There was an exciting story churning around in her head about a gang of crazy pirates who go off to see the king. The trouble was that if she wrote it, Miss Endicott would want her to take part in the play.

Reading was bad enough, but *acting!* Rebecca couldn't stand to think of it. She liked to do her talking with a pencil and then quit. But if she told Miss Endicott how she felt, she would probably just laugh her off. She'd say, "Whaaat? Why, David and Sarah would have loved the chance! Come on! It will do you good to get up in front of people."

She could always refuse to write the play. Or she could write such a stupid one that the teacher wouldn't want it. Probably she should do something about being so bashful. The further she went in school, the worse it got. What would happen when she got to high school?

What should Rebecca do?

Possible Discussion Topics:

1. Should Rebecca have to act in her play?
2. How can Rebecca explain she is different from her brother and sister so people will understand her better?
3. Why are some people bashful? Are there ways their classmates can help them?

WHAT SHOULD JOSHUA DO?

Josh is completely in the dark about decimals, but he doesn't want anyone to know for fear they will think he is stupid. Math class is getting more and more difficult.

Joshua glanced anxiously at the clock. Twenty minutes more before math would be over for the day. His heart pounded.

Mr. Kelly put down the chalk: "Any questions?"

Any questions! Josh had dozens. He seemed to be twice as slow to catch on as anybody else, and the worst of it was he didn't dare ask the teacher to explain anything for fear everyone would think he was terribly stupid. Last semester he had managed to wind up with a C in mathematics, but how he had had to work to do it!

A hand went up, and Mr. Kelly nodded: "John?"

"I understand how you find out what percent 12 is of 40, but if all you know is that 12 is 30 percent of *something*, how do you find what the something is?"

Josh's head reeled. What in the world was John talking about?

"A good question," Mr. Kelly said. "Think about it, class, and see if you can figure it out."

Josh had no idea what to do. He didn't even know how to begin. He could hear pencils scratching all around him. Soon, hands began to go up.

"All right, Maureen," Mr. Kelly said. "Go to the board and show us how you worked it."

Josh watched in bewilderment as the red-haired girl divided 12 by

.30. How did Maureen think of that? Where did she get the decimal? He tried to listen as Maureen explained what she was doing, but he couldn't follow the explanation. Was he the only one who couldn't get it?

"Is it clear to everyone now?" Mr. Kelly asked. "Jack, do you understand? . . . Susan? . . . Joshua?"

Josh's cheeks burned as he nodded. If he admitted he didn't understand, Mr. Kelly would make Maureen go over the problem again, and then what if Josh still couldn't understand?

"All right, let's go to the board and work out the problems on page 87. Ken, you take the first one; Joshua, the second. . . ."

Josh's knees felt as though they would buckle under him as he went to the board. Now the whole class would see how dumb he was, and Mr. Kelly would wonder why he had nodded that he understood. He couldn't go on like this. The longer he went without admitting that he didn't understand what decimals were all about, the worse it would get.

At that moment the fire bell rang. A fire drill. What a relief! But later it would be the same story all over again.

What should Joshua do?

Possible Discussion Topics:

1. Have you ever tried to bluff your way through a difficult subject? What happened?
2. Do kids in your school think you're dumb if you ask for help?
3. Have you ever laughed at someone who makes a mistake in class? How do you feel about kids who laugh at other's mistakes?

WHAT SHOULD GAIL DO?

Gail wants to be one of the "in" group, but has shabby clothes and feels she isn't very special. She's not interested in the other "outs" who are absorbed in music or science.

Gail sat alone, chewing on a dry peanut butter sandwich. It would have gone down more easily if she'd had an orange to go with it, but according to her mother, oranges were too expensive.

Gail watched a group of kids by the window. They were laughing at something going on on the playground. She would have given almost anything to be one of the group, but they never included her. You were "in" or you were "out," Gail decided miserably, and she was obviously "out."

To be popular in junior high school, you had to wear the kinds of clothes the other girls were wearing. Right now, the style at school was paisley prints. Gail not only didn't have a *paisley* print dress, she didn't have a print dress of any kind. All she had was one or two shabby skirts, a few blouses, and an old gray sweater—a hand-me-down from her aunt.

Just this morning, Gail had tried to explain to her mother how important it was for her to dress like the others.

"You don't have to tell me how it feels not to belong," Mother had said. "I never belonged to anything in my whole life. But no use crying over what you haven't got. You'll have to be liked for cheerfulness and things like that."

Gail didn't think she had much to be cheerful about. She wasn't pretty and she couldn't think of clever things to say. She didn't have any particular talent that she knew about. She was sure that even if she acted cheerful every minute, she still wouldn't be anything special.

Her classmates were nice enough, but they didn't let her in on their secrets or trade clothes with her or invite her home. Others in her class were "out" too, but this was apparently by choice. Some of them were honor students who liked to spend their time feeding the science animals or practicing for the orchestra. Gail didn't think she was smart enough to be "in" with them and she didn't think they were much fun anyway.

Poor Gail wanted desperately to belong to the popular group. What should she do?

Possible Discussion Topics:

1. How might Gail's resentment of her situation affect her behavior with others?
2. If Gail had the clothes she wanted, would she be sure of being "in"?
3. What could Gail learn from the girls who seemed "out" by choice?

WHAT SHOULD ARMANDO DO?

Armando's patrol duty is over and he's about to leave to finish his homework when he sees Lisa, who needs to cross safely to go home for lunch, turn back for something she forgot.

Armando stood on the corner in his yellow raincoat, his patrol belt damp from the wet snow. As soon as he was off duty, he told himself, he was going to get his arithmetic homework done before class. TV had been so interesting the night before that he hadn't finished doing his problems.

He checked traffic, saw that no cars were coming, and hurried a group of children across the road on their way home to lunch.

"That's the last of them," Armando said to himself. He looked at his watch and saw that in another minute or so he'd be off duty. Then he saw Lisa halfway down the hill from the school. The first grader was poking along, slushing through the snow.

"Hey, Lisa," Armando bellowed, "get a move on."

She walked a little faster, pausing only once to make a soggy snowball. Lisa was almost at the corner when she stopped short. "I forgot my Santa Claus picture," she wailed, and started trudging back up the hill.

"Lisa!" Armando yelled, "Come on. You can take your picture home this afternoon."

Lisa kept right on going back. Armando looked at his watch again. Officially, he was off duty. Why should he wait for Lisa? That little dope was so pokey that there was no telling how long it would take her to get back to the crossing, and Armando hated to think what Miss Cleaver would say if he didn't finish his arithmetic problems.

Armando was worried about leaving his corner, though. When Lisa got back to the crossing with her Santa Claus picture, could she get across the street safely without help? What if a car came whirling around the corner?

Armando made up his mind to wait for Lisa. Then he got to thinking no one would ever find out that he knew Lisa would be coming back, whereas Miss Cleaver would most certainly find out that he had goofed off on his homework if he didn't get busy on it right away. What should Armando do?

Possible Discussion Topics:

1. What mistake had Armando made that really caused his whole problem?
2. Was Armando's responsibility for safety over when he was officially off duty?
3. If Armando had not been on the safety patrol, would he have had any responsibility to wait for Lisa?

WHAT SHOULD KELLY DO?

Kelly's dying to win first prize in the art contest but knows that Evelyn's painting—her only real competition—is about to be ruined in the rain.

"It's beautiful, whether you win first place or not."

That's what Mother said when Kelly showed her the painting she'd done for the school art contest. But Mother put it differently to Aunt Lois.

"She really has talent, Lois," Kelly heard her say on the phone. "I'll certainly be disappointed if she doesn't win first prize."

Kelly would be disappointed herself, in a way. She was almost the best artist in the whole school. Almost. Of course, there was always Evelyn Fields.

When Evelyn felt like painting, she could turn out pictures that looked good enough to be on magazine covers, but she only painted when and what she wanted to. She had said over and over again that she couldn't care less about prizes and contests and rules.

The art teacher certainly cared about rules, though. "Last year," she said, "I spent half my time reminding students of the deadline and rounding up paintings on time. This year each person is responsible for his own painting. Anyone whose picture isn't in the office by nine-thirty Friday morning is out of luck."

On the day of the contest, Kelly, with her painting carefully wrapped in brown paper, waited on the school steps for the bell to ring. Evelyn arrived, propped a picture against the side of the school, and hurried over to the swings.

Kelly looked at Evelyn's picture. Evelyn certainly must have felt like painting this time, for the picture was the best she'd ever done—horses on the desert, and a fiery sun in the background casting a red glow over the entire landscape. Evelyn was sure to win first prize whether she wanted to or not.

Kelly could hardly hold back the tears. When the bell rang, she turned her picture in at the office and went to the fifth-grade room. The teacher assigned some arithmetic examples. Kelly broke her pencil on the first one, so she went to the sharpener by the window. As she was grinding away, some drops splattered against the glass. Kelly looked out and saw that it was raining. She saw something else, too.

There, right where Evelyn had left it, was the splendid horse picture. In five minutes, it would be too late for Evelyn to enter her picture in the contest, and Kelly would probably win. Kelly looked quickly at Evelyn, but the other girl was hard at work on a problem.

Well, she's got to learn to take care of her own things, Kelly told herself. The teacher said we were each responsible for our own painting, so Evelyn's responsible for hers. That's the rule. It's her tough luck if she doesn't win first prize.

But that wasn't the only problem. A few more minutes in the rain and the painting would be ruined. That would hurt Evelyn a lot more than losing the contest.

Kelly went back to her seat with her heart pounding. What should she do?

Possible Discussion Topics:

1. Since being responsible for one's own painting is a contest rule, would it be fair for Kelly to remind Evelyn that she hasn't turned hers in?
2. Would winning first prize mean as much to Kelly if she won because Evelyn's picture was ruined as it would if she won in a real competition?
3. Do you think school contests are a good idea? Why do you feel the way you do?

WHAT SHOULD ANDY DO?

The school cafeteria cashier has given Andy one dollar too much in change and he knows it.

When Andy set his tray on the table he realized that he had given the cashier at the lunch counter a $5-bill for a lunch that cost 40¢ and received five $1-bills and 60¢ in return.

He stared at the money in his hand, then back at Mrs. Laster, the cashier, who was busy counting out change for someone else and didn't realize that Andy had a dollar too much.

Andy sat down at the table and put $4.60 in his wallet. Maybe I'll wait until there's no line and then go give the dollar back, he thought. Still, it wasn't his fault that the cashier made a mistake. If she was so careless, then maybe she ought to get cheated now and then.

He bit into his hamburger, thinking hard. He wasn't used to having so much money, but just this morning his dad had given him the $5 and said, "Let's see how well you can handle this much money, Andy." Well, the extra dollar would certainly make it easier to prove to his dad that he could make his money last.

Anyway, I'll bet it will all even out in the end, he told himself. The cashier will probably make the mistake the other way sometime and charge me too much. Then we'll be even. Or maybe the cashier has charged me too much before and I haven't even noticed it! Maybe the cashier overcharged me two or three times!

Besides, think of all the times I've been cheated by the cafeteria—the time I didn't get pickles with my barbecue, or the day my piece of pie was only half the size of the others, or the time my slice of pizza was burned on the bottom. I'm just getting what's coming to me, that's all. I ought to keep the dollar and forget it.

But somehow Andy couldn't forget it. He kept asking himself, Is it really wrong to keep the dollar or not? What should Andy do?

Possible Discussion Topics:

1. If Andy feels cheated now and then on a cafeteria item, what should he do?
2. Would Andy think it fair if the cashier kept a dollar he had overpaid accidentally?
3 Is it possible to be dishonest by keeping silent?

WHAT SHOULD EMILY DO?

Emily has befriended a handicapped girl who now wants to spend every recess with her. Emily doesn't want to hurt her feelings but wants to play with her other friends, too.

Emily wanted to be kind to Lois, but there were times she wished she hadn't ever spoken to her in the first place.

It started several weeks ago when the special education class began having recess at the same time as the fourth graders. Most of the children in this class had some form of brain damage. Because they were not able to learn as quickly as other children, they were taught by a special teacher, and Emily had not seen much of them until they began coming out to recess.

Most of the special education pupils played by themselves on the front steps, but one girl, a little older than the others, always sat on the swings and watched Emily and her friends jumping rope. She looked so lonely and forlorn that one day Emily called, "Why don't you come over and jump too?"

"Oh, Emily, for heaven's sake, not *her!*" Jean said.

"Why not?" Emily said. "She's been sitting there all week watching. She'd probably love it."

And Lois did. She was terribly awkward at it, and consequently the other girls didn't get much of a turn, but her beaming face told Emily how much fun she was having.

The next day Lois was back, eagerly waiting her turn, and the next day and the next. Finally, Jean and the other girls went off to play by themselves, leaving Emily and Lois alone on the swings.

Lois didn't seem to mind, however. She was grateful for Emily's attention and was content just to talk to her in her slow stammering way.

Now every recess, twice a day, Lois was waiting when Emily came out, her face so eager that Emily didn't dare let her down. She wanted to stay friends with Lois, but she wanted time to be with the other kids, too. The trouble was that when Lois was around, they simply couldn't do the things they usually did without having her interfere.

What should Emily do?

Possible Discussion Topics:

1. Why do handicapped children have a special need for friends?

2. Since Emily decided to be friendly to Lois, does she have a duty to spend all her time with her, every recess?
3. How could Emily get the other girls to play part of the time with Lois?

WHAT SHOULD JONATHAN DO?

Things are out-of-hand for the substitute teacher, Miss Evans. Jonathan feels sorry for her and wants to help, but he doesn't want to be called a teacher's pet.

As Jonathan entered the classroom, he started to say, "May I feed the fish, Miss Schwartz?" but he stopped. Instead of Miss Schwartz, a different teacher, a younger woman, was at the desk, busily studying the plan book.

"Miss Schwartz is ill today," the new teacher said when everybody was seated. "I'm Miss Evans. I do hope we'll get along well together."

Her voice sounded real funny, as if she were talking through her nose. Jonathan heard Bill Brown, in the back of the room, softly mimic, "I *do* hope we'll get along well together." Somebody started to snicker.

Miss Evans seemed not to have heard, because she picked up the roll book and started to call off names. When she came to Mike Moretti's name, she pronounced it "Mike Mor-eet-i." This made everybody laugh. Miss Evans' face got pink, but she kept on. When she called Ray Parker, who was absent, Bill disguised his voice and said, "Here," and Miss Evans marked him present. A lot of kids snickered that time.

As the morning wore on, things grew worse. Miss Evans asked where the workbooks were, and the kids in the back kept telling her the wrong cupboard. This made everyone start giggling.

Next, Carlotta said that Miss Schwartz always let them walk around the room at ten o'clock so they could stretch their legs. She was fibbing, but Miss Evans let them do it. This seemed like such a funny joke that everybody laughed and giggled some more.

By this time, Miss Evans was upset. Jonathan could tell by the way the pink stayed in her cheeks. She was having a really hard time. She didn't know anybody's name or where anything was, and the class—with Bill Brown leading the way—was getting her all mixed up.

It wasn't right. Jonathan felt that he should do something about it, but he didn't want to be called a teacher's pet. And after all, teachers ought to be able to take care of themselves, shouldn't they?

At eleven o'clock, someone told Miss Evans that they were supposed to see a moving picture. This wasn't true, for they had seen the movie the day before, so when Miss Evans started to get out the projector and the film, everyone began laughing again.

Something should be done, Jonathan thought. What should he do?

Possible Discussion Topics:

1. What are some of the things you can think of that Jonathan can do to help Miss Evans?
2. If you were in the class, how do you think you would act?
3. What are some of the problems and feelings teachers have that students ought to be aware of?

WHAT SHOULD THE CLASS DO?

When the kids learn about the personal problem that has been making their teacher crosser and crosser, they want to make up for their bad behavior.

When school started in September, Miss Hurley had had a twinkle in her eye that meant she was ready for a good laugh, and the projects she introduced were usually interesting to do.

By the time January rolled around, however, Miss Hurley had lost the twinkle, and her voice seemed strangely sharp. Sometimes the smallest things seemed to annoy her.

As the weeks went by, she grew crosser and crosser. She would get so angry so easily that it got to be funny. Some of the children did things they knew they shouldn't do, just to see the explosion.

"Boy, she's changed," somebody said.

"Yeah, from wonderful to witch," answered someone else.

One morning Bobby Edleston, who had previously been acting worse than almost anyone else, was the best-behaved boy in the class. At recess he whispered to some of his friends, "Hey, you guys, I think we ought to lay off of Miss Hurley. Mom just found out that Miss Hurley's only sister is in the hospital, and she's awfully sick." He went on to tell them that every day, right after school, Miss Hurley drove to the hospital and stayed there with her sister until late at night. Of course, after she got home, she still had to grade papers and plan the next day's work before she could go to bed.

Bobby's mother had explained that Miss Hurley couldn't just stay out of school until her sister was better, because she had to keep working so that she could pay hospital and doctor bills.

After the other children had heard Bobby's story, they started to think of things they had seen that should have made them realize that something was really bothering Miss Hurley. Her eyes often looked red, as if she'd been crying, and one morning when Bobby and a friend came into the classroom early they found Miss Hurley with her head down on the desk fast asleep.

Somehow the children had never thought of what Miss Hurley's life was like outside the classroom. They had never even imagined that she or any of the other teachers had problems and worries or aches and pains of their own. But the class knew better now. And as they remembered how upset Miss Hurley had been all these weeks and how they had behaved, they felt bad and wanted somehow to make it up to her. What should Miss Hurley's class do?

Possible Discussion Topics:

1. How do you act toward others when you are worried about something? Are you as kind and thoughtful and patient as you are at other times?
2. How is teaching different from many other jobs? Is the teacher's work over once the children leave the classroom?
3. What would Miss Hurley appreciate most?

WHAT SHOULD GEORGE DO?

George feels burdened by his handicapped older brother who tags after him at school.

George was in fifth grade, and somewhat large for his age. Kevin, his brother, was two years older and even bigger than George. Both boys went to Spring Valley School, but Kevin was in the special class for handicapped children. Like some of the other boys and girls in the class, as a child Kevin had had a serious illness that injured his brain. As a result, he had difficulty with his schoolwork and moved his arms and legs awkwardly.

Until this year, Kevin had been taught at home by a visiting teacher. But he had improved so much that the teacher felt he should now attend the special class. So every day, George had to walk Kevin to school, and every day he wished he didn't have to.

Many of George's friends at school hadn't known until now that he even had a brother. Always before, Kevin had preferred to stay in the house and play, and so he had never been much of a problem to George.

But he was now. The big school frightened Kevin, and he tagged along after George like a puppy. No matter what George did outside the classroom, if it was climbing the monkey bars or playing baseball, Kevin was there making a nuisance of himself. Once he fell off the monkey bars and cut his lip. Another time he followed George to second base and collided with the shortstop. Worst of all was the way Kevin walked and talked and moved his hands. George was used to this, but the other kids weren't, and George couldn't get used to the way they laughed and pointed at Kevin.

As the days went by, George resented Kevin more and more. He tried to ignore him, refused to answer him, and even hid sometimes when he saw him coming at lunchtime or recess. The other kids joined in and made a game of it—hiding from Kevin or teasing him by sending him on a wild-goose chase after George. One time Kevin even started to bawl, and George laughed at him right along with the others.

He didn't feel good about it, though. He'd always liked his big, awkward brother. He admired the persistent way Kevin went about things, sometimes taking several minutes to tie one shoe but never once complaining. And he appreciated the generous way Kevin shared anything at all with him.

But George wanted to be a part of things at school, too. He wanted to have friends and not be stuck with Kevin all the time. What should George do?

Possible Discussion Topics:

1. Is laughing at someone sometimes a cover-up for not knowing what else to do?
2. How might George interest his friends in helping Kevin instead of teasing him?
3. What do people with Kevin's handicap need?

WHAT SHOULD FRANK DO?

Frank has never been to the zoo, but if he goes with his class there will be no one to care for his little brother after school.

Frank lived over on 128th Street with his mother and his little brother, Benny. His mother had to work every day, so Frank was used to looking out for Benny.

The boys walked to and from school together, and Frank always hung on to Benny to keep him from dashing out into the street. It wasn't easy. Benny was always wanting to do something on the other side of the street—look in a store window or pat some mangy cat he saw over there. Sometimes Benny broke away and Frank would have to chase after him. When that happened, sometimes both brothers would be late for school.

One Friday morning, though, the boys got to school in plenty of time. Frank took his little brother to the first-grade room and shoved him inside. If he didn't make sure that Benny was in the room, the little boy might go wandering around in the halls.

"That kid hasn't got sense enough to come in out of the rain," Frank muttered to himself as he walked to his own room.

The fourth graders seemed excited and lots of the kids were dressed up. Frank suddenly remembered that this was the day Miss Raymond was going to take the class to the zoo. How could he have forgotten? Everybody said the zoo was wonderful. Mom had often said she'd take him and Benny someday, but she never seemed to have time.

Suddenly he remembered Benny! The class wouldn't get back from the zoo until four o'clock, half an hour after everyone else had been dismissed. Who would see that Benny got home all right? Suppose he tried to go by himself! If he managed to get there without being run over, who would look after him?

Frank wanted to go to the zoo so much he ached, but what about Benny? Frank wondered if his teacher would let his little brother go to the zoo with the fourth grade. But what if she said no? What should Frank do?

Possible Discussion Topics:

1. Does looking after a younger brother or sister sometimes interfere with what you want to do? How does it make you feel?

2. Does Frank have any other choices for Benny after school?

3. What is more important, the zoo or Benny?

WHAT SHOULD PETE DO?

Pete jumps to the conclusion that Keith stole their teacher's pen and tells the class. Later he learns that he is wrong.

Miss Iannucci's new pen was missing. The children had admired it when she had used it to take the roll that morning and she had told them that her brother had sent it to her from Japan. She had let the class pass it from one person to another so that everyone could look at the ship floating mysteriously in liquid inside the cap. Now the pen was gone. Miss Iannucci asked everybody to look in their desk to see if it might be there by mistake.

"I'll bet somebody took it," Pete said to his friends at recess. And all during the game of soft ball, he kept wondering who might have done it.

Suddenly, he saw a girl's silver locket lying in the grass. "I'm going to take this in," he called to the others, and hurried toward the principal's office. At the office door, he stopped. Mr. Myers, the principal, was talking quietly, but very seriously, to Keith Bronson. Keith, with his face a mottled red, was standing by the desk, looking almost ready to cry. Pete quickly dropped the locket into the lost and found box and ran back outdoors.

"Listen!" he called to his friends. "I'll bet anything that Keith Bronson took Miss Iannucci's pen. The principal was bawling him out about something, and wow, did old Keith look sick!"

"Sure," said Alex. "He made more fuss over the pen than anybody, and all the time he was going to take it home, the robber!"

When the kids took their seats after recess, they frowned at Keith to let him know that they knew. Keith looked puzzled for a minute and then his face turned red again.

He's the one, all right, Pete thought.

After school when Pete was helping to clean blackboards, he was not surprised to see the pen back on Miss Iannucci's desk.

"Oh, you have your pen again!" he said to the teacher.

"Yes, I found it between the pages of the roll book," Miss Iannucci laughed.

Pete stood still. "You... you found it in the roll book?" he stammered.

"Yes, wasn't that silly? I must have closed the book on it."

Pete didn't answer. Slowly he finished washing the blackboard. His cheeks felt hot. By now, almost everyone in the class thought Keith was a thief, and it wasn't true. Whatever Keith had been upset about in the principal's office, it wasn't about the pen. In fact, Pete was not even sure Mr. Myers had been scolding Keith.

Well, what of it? Pete tried to tell himself. I didn't say for sure that he took it. I said I bet he had because I thought Mr. Myers was bawling him out, and that much was true.

But Pete didn't feel any better. He was the one who had started the rumor. Now what should he do?

Possible Discussion Topics:

1. Would Pete feel better if he apologized to Keith? Would Keith?
2. Why are rumors so hurtful to those involved?
3. Have you ever felt like Pete after telling about something you saw or heard? Tell about it.

WHAT SHOULD NORMAN DO?

Norman can't stand David and sees a chance to start some gossip that might embarrass him.

If there was one person on his whole block and in the whole school Norman didn't like, it was David Overby. Whatever David wanted—a $75 bike, a prize at the science fair, a place on the basketball team—he got. As for Norman, he got to be a reporter on the sixth-grade newsletter, and that was all. Big deal.

OK, so he was jealous, Norman admitted to himself. That wasn't all, though. David had a stuck-up way about him that others disliked too, and most of the kids wished that the next time David won first prize at the science fair, it would be a scholarship to a school a hundred miles away.

Then one evening about nine o'clock, Norman noticed a police car parked across the street in front of Overbys', its light flashing. He could hardly believe it. A robbery? A fight, maybe? How neat it would be if David were in some trouble.

"Somebody over at Overbys' is getting arrested," Norman said.

"Don't jump to conclusions," his father answered, settling back in his armchair. "Maybe one of the officers is a friend of the family. It's not our business, anyway."

In the morning, Norman saw David walking to school. Perhaps he just imagined it, but David looked sheepish about something, as though he didn't want anyone to know about the police being at his house.

Dad was wrong about its not being my business, Norman thought. *Everything* is a reporter's business. That's my job.

Of course, Norman realized that he couldn't put an article in the newsletter about seeing the police car at the Overbys', but he might just mention it to a few people. All he would be doing was stating a fact, so it wouldn't be as if he were starting gossip, and it seemed to him like a good way to get even with David. Still, he knew his father would think it was wrong. He was puzzled. What should Norman do?

Possible Discussion Topics:

1. If Norman had seen a police car at someone else's house, would he be so eager to tell about it?
2. Is it true that he would not be starting any gossip just by stating the facts?
3. Does a newspaper reporter have any responsibility to protect a person from gossip?

WHAT SHOULD GLORIA DO?

Gloria didn't trip Charlene on purpose but the teacher thinks she did and punishes her. Gloria is angry and feels she must do something.

Gloria's cheeks burned, but the rest of the class was laughing. Even Charlene, sprawled on the floor with the tray of paint jars, was laughing.

Gloria had been reading her science book and hadn't even noticed Charlene going by until she felt something hit her foot and heard the crash of the paint jars.

"You and your big feet!" Charlene yelled as she hit the floor, and everybody roared.

But this was the last straw for Miss Kanoho. Everything had gone wrong all day long. She decided that Gloria had tripped Charlene on purpose, and so she announced that Gloria was to stay indoors at recess for one week.

Gloria wanted to explain, but she just sat there "opening and closing her mouth like a goldfish" as one of her friends laughed afterwards. It wasn't so much the punishment. It was the humiliation of being scolded in front of the class.

All afternoon Gloria burned inside. She could hardly speak when Miss Kanoho asked her a question in arithmetic. Never before had she felt so angry and helpless.

It's so unfair, she thought. I'll get even. I won't do another thing for her as long as I live. And when Valentine's Day comes, she sure won't get a card from me!

At the end of the day, Gloria purposely banged down the lid of her desk so Miss Kanoho would know she was mad at her and marched out the door. At supper that night she hardly ate a thing. Finally, at their urging, she told her family what was wrong.

"Shoot her!" cried Gloria's little brother, Jimmy. Gloria almost laughed, but she was too upset to do even that.

"Report it to the principal," her other brother said.

"Well, do *something*," Mother put in. "Don't just stew about it." It was hard for Gloria to get rid of a grudge. Maybe she was taking it all too seriously. The rest of the class had thought it was funny. But it was no joke to her. She was really angry and had to get it off her chest. What should she do?

Possible Discussion Topics:

1. Is it bad to just "stew about things"? Why?
2. Would getting even make her feel better? Would going to Miss Kanoho and explaining?
3. How do you feel when a teacher, or one of your parents, says you did something you did not do?

WHAT SHOULD PEGGY DO?

Peggy joins the other kids watching the principal search for the keys to her car. She knows Dick found them, but she promised not to tell.

It's a secret!"

Peggy could see Joan waving at her from across the school yard. She smiled to herself. Joan was so crazy. She was always thinking up silly things to do, and everyone liked her—and loved her secrets!

Once Joan had hidden a live chicken in her desk. Another time she had passed around rubber cookies that looked like real ones. So when she called out that she had another secret, Peggy hurried over.

"Promise you won't tell," demanded Joan.

"Oh yes, I promise I won't tell," said Peggy.

"Cross your heart and hope to die?" Joan asked solemnly.

"Cross my heart and hope to die."

"Raise five fingers to the sky and say you'll sass your mother," Joan instructed.

Wow! This was serious. Peggy raised one hand and promised to sass her mother if she ever dared tell the secret. "Okay," Joan leaned over and cupped her hand to Peggy's ear. "Dick Everly found Mrs. Kreeger's car keys and has them in his pocket."

Peggy's mouth dropped open. The principal's keys!

"He's going to give them to her, isn't he?"

"Of course not. That will be half the fun, watching her hunt for them. We're going to stay here on the swings after school and see what happens."

The school bell rang as Peggy opened her mouth to answer. As they ran toward the building, Joan said, "Remember, you *promised*."

All through social studies, Peggy wondered about those keys. Maybe Dick would change his mind. Maybe when it came time to go home he'd give the keys to the principal.

When the last bell rang, Peggy went out to the swings where Joan was waiting. Pretty soon Dick and some other kids came running over. Peggy could tell from the look on Dick's face that he still had the keys. She felt uncomfortable.

A few minutes later Mrs. Kreeger came outside. She started walking slowly around the building, looking in the grass and peering down under her car. Joan and Dick and the others were laughing themselves sick, but Peggy was strangely silent.

This wasn't funny at all. How would the principal get home? What if she had an important appointment? Peggy was worried.

But she had promised not to tell. What should Peggy do?

Possible Discussion Topics:

1. Should Peggy just have gone home and forgotten all about the principal and the keys?
2. How could Peggy talk Dick into giving the keys back to Mrs. Kreeger?
3. What would happen if Peggy just walked over and told Mrs. Kreeger who had the keys?

WHAT SHOULD CAROL DO?

Carol is new in school and lonely. She sees a chance to get in good with Janey, the most popular girl in her room, but it means letting someone else get blamed for Janey's misdeed.

Carol walked slowly across the playground toward the entrance, a lonely little figure at the end of the stream of lively children returning to class after recess. Oh, how she wished they had never moved from Spring Street School! The children here were so unfriendly—none of the kids in her room had said anything more than "Hi" to her, and it didn't look as though anyone would.

Back at Spring Street, she and her best friend, Ellen, had been a welcome part of everything that went on in fourth grade. She missed Ellen badly, but even more she missed the warm, comfortable feeling that people liked her. Here at Highland she might as well be invisible.

Just ahead of her, next-to-the-last one in, was Janey Wells, who sat across the aisle. Janey was the most popular girl in Mrs. Tucker's room, and if she liked you, your troubles were over. If she didn't—well, too bad for you. A delightful picture of herself walking arm in arm with Janey grew in Carol's mind. They would be whispering together, and laughing together, and the whole class would see that Carol was fun, and kids would ask her to play after school, and . . . and . . .

Suddenly Carol saw Janey pull a paper—it looked like a page from a book—from her jacket pocket and push it down into the center of the half-filled trash can that stood just outside the building. Janey looked quickly around. When she saw Carol, her face turned red, and she ran ahead into the classroom.

Mrs. Tucker was really upset that afternoon when she opened the atlas to refer to something on the detailed map of Utah and found half the page missing. "Don, you were the last one to use the atlas. What happened to this map?"

The more Don said he didn't know anything about it, the more exasperated Mrs. Tucker became. Finally, she said, "We won't waste any more class time talking about this now, young man; we'll continue the discussion after three o'clock."

Don was always having to stay after. He was noisy, and he pushed people; only yesterday he had made Carol fall at recess. This time he'd get sent to the principal for sure! It served him right.

But suddenly Carol remembered—Janey had been using the atlas first thing that morning. She must have torn it accidentally and then thrown the page into the trash so that no one would know. Carol stole a glance across the aisle, and there was Janey signaling, "Don't tell!"

What should Carol do? Should she do what Janey wanted and not say anything? Actually, how could she be sure what it was that Janey didn't want her to tell? Still, she had a definite feeling that if she kept quiet, Janey would begin to act friendly, and the others always followed Janey's lead. Should she tell Mrs. Tucker what she had seen and let her decide what to do? The kids would think she was a tattletale; and besides, Don was a pest. But was it fair to let him be punished if he hadn't done anything wrong? What should she do?

Possible Discussion Topics:
1. Do you think Carol would have been a tattletale if she told Mrs. Tucker what she saw?
2. Would Carol have been happy if she kept quiet and Janey started acting friendly as a result?
3. If things had happened in reverse and Janey were suspected instead of Don, what do you think Carol should have done?

WHAT SHOULD TYRONE DO?

After Tyrone sees his little brother throw a rock through the cafeteria window he hears him tell the principal that another student did it.

Unlike lots of kids, Tyrone was crazy about his little brother. Not only was he the cutest little guy in the second grade, but he was always telling wild tales that made him laugh.

It was fun for sixth-grader Tyrone to meet Charlie in the hall, or watch him on the playground, or peep into the second-grade room where he sat with his little sneakered feet tucked under his chair.

One afternoon at recess, Tyrone and some other sixth graders were making mats out of dandelion stems for a social studies project. Tyrone had gone around the side of the building to get more dandelions when the bell rang. Just as he turned the corner, he saw his little brother pick up a big rock, throw it through the cafeteria window, and scurry to the back of the building.

Although no one else was in sight outdoors, Tyrone felt that someone inside the building would certainly have seen Charlie break the window and report it to the principal. He went to his room, but was so worried about Charlie that he finally asked his teacher for permission to leave the room. He went to the office prepared to stand by his little brother during what he was sure would be an unpleasant interview.

When he got to the office, sure enough, there was Charlie talking to the principal. He didn't look unhappy, however.

When he saw him, he said cheerfully, "Hi, Tyrone. I'm telling Mr. Garcia how I saw Michael Lansing throw a rock through the cafeteria window."

"Michael Lansing!" Tyrone said.

Charlie nodded. "He just picked up a big stone and—pow—right through the window. Miss King asked if anybody knew about the window, so I told her, and she sent me to tell Mr. Garcia."

Tyrone knew Michael Lansing. He was always getting into trouble. But this was one thing he hadn't done. He had seen Charlie throw the rock, and now, to make matters worse, he had made up a deliberate lie about it.

He hated to think what the principal would say to Charlie if he learned the truth, and he hated to imagine how their parents would punish his brother when they heard the story. Of course, Charlie had done two very bad things and deserved to be punished, but was it up to Tyrone to tell on him? It certainly wasn't fair for Michael Lansing to be blamed, but how he hated to be the one to get Charlie into trouble. What should Tyrone do?

Possible Discussion Topics:

1. Would Tyrone be helping his brother if he lets him get away with putting the blame on Michael?
2. What if Michael had broken the window and said Charlie did it; what would Tyrone do then?
3. What would your parents expect you to do if you were in Tyrone's place?

WHAT SHOULD SUSIE DO?

In a moment of anger, Susie wrote a composition, "I hate my mother because...." She regrets it, but if she asks for it back she won't have time to write another and might get a D.

"Ugh. Homely, scratchy old sweater," Susie thought, and kicked at a rock. She kicked too hard and hurt her foot. As she went limping into the school, Susie decided that the sore foot was her mother's fault—if her mother hadn't made her mad by insisting that she wear this ugly grey cardigan on a warm spring day, she wouldn't have kicked the rock.

Susie still felt twinges in her foot when she got to the fourth-grade room, and even though she had hung her sweater in the locker, she still felt hot and itchy.

"Please hand in your arithmetic homework," said Miss Sanchez when the last bell sounded. "I'm going to go over it particularly carefully because I have to turn in grades for report cards tomorrow, and some of you are just on the border between one mark and another."

"Well," thought Susie, "that means I'll get an A. I've had almost all A's and when Daddy checked my arithmetic last night, he said I had all the answers right." She opened the black notebook on her desk. It wasn't hers! This was her little brother's! Now she wouldn't get an A in arithmetic, Susie thought, and it would be all her mother's fault for buying Bud a notebook just like Susie's. "Dumb old Mom," Susie muttered to herself.

All during arithmetic, Susie grew crosser and crosser.

Composition followed arithmetic. Miss Sanchez assigned the subject, "I Like ———— Because."

Like? Susie decided she didn't like anybody. She borrowed a piece of paper from the person in front of her and wrote, "I hate my mother because," and then she wrote all the ways in which her mother seemed to be unfair or unreasonable or just plain mean.

At ten-thirty, when it was time to go out to recess, Susie stopped by her locker to get a ball that she had put in her sweater pocket. As she got out the ball, a little waxed paper package popped out along with it. Inside were two homemade cookies. Mom must have put them there to make her feel better about wearing the sweater.

As she munched on the cookies, Susie wondered what dessert her mother would fix for dinner tonight. That got her too; thinking how her mother was always planning surprises for the family—like special desserts and buying that notebook for Bud. Mom really didn't make her dress warmly just to be mean, but because she knew how likely Susie was to catch a bad cold in the spring. She was really O.K. as a mother.

Susie wished now that she'd never written that composition. When Miss Sanchez read it, she'd think Susie had an awful mother. Susie decided to ask Miss Sanchez to return the composition without reading it. Then she realized that there wasn't time to write another one, and she might get a D on her report card if she had only a blank space in the record book in the place where the mark on the composition ought to be.

What should Susie do?

Possible Discussion Topics:

1. Was Susie's mother to blame for Susie's troubles?
2. Would reading the composition really make Miss Sanchez believe that Susie had "an awful mother"?
3. What made Susie get over being cross? Was it the cookies, the thoughts of dessert for dinner, or something entirely different?

WHAT SHOULD BENNY DO?

Benny and Paul aren't speaking when Mrs. Harris chooses them to work together on a weather station, something they would both like to do.

Everybody knew it, though Mrs. Harris acted as if she didn't: Benny and Paul weren't speaking. They couldn't even stand the sight of each other. When Paul told Benny he'd never speak to him again, he'd meant it. And when Benny said he was glad to hear it, he had meant that just as much.

Now, of all things, Mrs. Harris had chosen Paul and Benny to work together on planning and setting up a weather station.

"If I have to sit and look at *him*, I'll get sick," Benny told his friends.

The boys had quarreled a week ago, and it seemed as though the longer they were enemies, the more they disliked each other. Paul had really started the feud by calling Benny names because he got mad at something he thought Benny had said that Benny hadn't said at all.

Then instead of explaining to Paul, Benny had flared up because Paul called him bad names. Pretty soon all of Benny's friends were mad at Paul's friends, and nobody knew what was true and what wasn't.

"I won't do it! I can't work with him!" Benny muttered as he threw on his windbreaker and started home for lunch. But someplace inside of himself he wasn't sure.

Benny figured that Mrs. Harris had appointed Paul and him to make the weather station because they both were interested in the weather and both of them were good in science. Also, Benny had already started work on an anemometer. She must have forgotten the fight, Benny thought. But how could he and Paul work together if they weren't speaking?

Benny thought of the things he could do. He could tell Mrs. Harris he wouldn't work with Paul. Perhaps he could work on the project alone, and then when Paul didn't help, he could tell her that Paul wasn't cooperating. Of course, he could apologize to Paul, but why should he when Paul had started the whole thing?

Benny knew he had to do something. With half of the kids mad at him and the other half mad at Paul, it was beginning to look as though nobody in the class would get anything done if the two of them didn't make up. What should Benny do?

Possible Discussion Topics:

1. Should Benny give up something he really wants to do because of pride?
2. Why is it that so many arguments that cause so much trouble start over simple misunderstandings?
3. What could the class do to help Benny and Paul start speaking again?

WHAT SHOULD GWENDOLYN DO?

Gwen's disgusted with herself because she's never able to put her feelings into words.

"... So Gwen and Tony and Carmela may go to the study room and practice their play. The rest of you will work on your special projects here."

Mrs. Brunner put down the chalk and her eye caught Gwen's. "Is anything wrong, Gwen?"

Everything's wrong, Gwen wanted to answer. Instead, however, her cheeks flushed and her throat tightened and she said quickly, "No, Ma'am."

She'd done it again. She couldn't speak up. She'd even been asked point blank, but she simply couldn't put her feelings into words. Gwendolyn opened her desk and took out the play that she and Tony and Carmela were rehearsing for the fifth-grade program.

Tony and Carmela had already left the room, and Gwendolyn followed them slowly down the hall. All she would have had to say was, "I don't think we need any more practice, Mrs. Brunner. We know it well enough now." That's all. Of course, the other two would have glared at her, but she'd have felt better to have said what she felt. Instead, she would spend another boring hour listening to Tony and Carmela giggle and cut up when she would far rather be doing something else. But how was Mrs. Brunner to know if no one told her?

This one time wouldn't matter so much, Gwen decided glumly, if she hadn't been afraid to speak up a hundred times before. Whenever Gwen was asked an opinion, she clammed up. Whenever she disagreed inside, she agreed on the outside. Whenever her head said, "No," her mouth said, "Yes." And whenever it happened, she hated herself a little more.

It was a problem she couldn't even discuss with her parents. Mother reacted exactly the same way as Gwen, and Dad was even worse. The two never argued about anything. If they disagreed, they merely stopped talking for a while until finally the disagreement got pushed aside without their ever talking it out.

So Gwen had never really learned to express herself. She wished desperately that she could speak up the way the other children did. But how could she learn to do it? What should Gwendolyn do?

Possible Discussion Topics:

1. Is it true that we usually behave much as our parents do?
2. What are one or two steps Gwen might take on her own toward speaking up?
3. What are some of the reactions Gwendolyn might get when she first begins expressing her honest opinions? How might she handle them?

WHAT SHOULD BRUCE DO?

Bruce plays the patsy in order to be liked. He senses that it's not working so well.

Bruce looked longingly at Sid's chocolate ice cream cone, but he spent his own dessert money on candy that he could share with the other boys. Wouldn't it be neat, he thought, if there were something about me that would make people like me even if I didn't keep doing things for them all the time.

Bruce had never been able to think of anything that people could like about him so he went through life doing things that would make people act as though they liked him.

For instance, he always offered to lend his homework to people who hadn't done theirs, and he'd give up his turn at bat when recess was almost over if someone wanted an extra turn. If one of the kids had to clean the garage on Saturday, Bruce would help, even though he'd rather be playing ball. Whenever anybody asked a favor of Bruce, he obliged—in fact, he usually volunteered before he was asked.

"Good old Bruce," the fellows would say, "I knew you'd do it." Or just, "Attaboy, Bruce!"

In spite of what the kids said, Bruce felt sure they were laughing at him behind his back. In fact, he had a feeling that they probably disliked him because he was such a soft touch. He even hated himself because he acted the way he did. Then he'd say to himself, "Oh, well, at least they can't say I never do anything for anybody. It's better than being like Sam or Eddy, who never want to share anything with anybody and always have some excuse for not helping anybody."

That didn't help him feel much better, though. He wished he could change, but he was afraid that if he quit doing things for the kids they probably wouldn't even say hello to him. What should Bruce do?

Possible Discussion Topics:
1. Is it possible that Bruce might have just as many friends if he stopped doing favors unless they involved doing something he really wanted to do?
2. How could Bruce start refusing requests and still let the kids know that he wanted to be friendly?
3. If Bruce really wants to change, where might he turn for help?

WHAT SHOULD LARRY DO?

Larry keeps doing things with the crowd because he doesn't want to appear different. But, he'd really like to be himself.

Larry stood watching the chameleon in the pet store window. Only a minute before, it had been as gray as the piece of bark it was crawling on. Now, stretched out on a leaf, it was green. Wherever the chameleon was, it blended in so well with its background that you'd scarcely have seen it if you hadn't known it was there.

"I'm like that," Larry told himself, too disgusted even to look at his reflection in the glass. "That's what I am, a chameleon. I keep acting like the rest of the gang even when I don't want to, just so I won't stand out. The worst of it is, I made up my mind the first day of school that I would be myself this year."

Every morning last year, Larry's crowd had met outside of school early, and spent the time before school mimicking the teachers or teasing other kids or telling jokes. Now the gang was starting off the same way as before. Sometimes Larry got a kick out of it. Peter Kimball's imitation of old Mr. Leery was a riot—even Mr. Leery laughed at it. And some of the kids laughed and acted pleased over the teasing. Before long, though, the gang's antics had grown pretty boring to Larry. There were lots of other ways he'd rather spend the time before the bell rang.

Take today. What Larry really wanted to when he got to school was go straight to the library and read what the encyclopedia had to say about fossils. He had found a rock that seemed to have a leaf etched right into it. His father had said he thought it was a fossil, and Larry wanted to see if he could find out for sure.

In Larry's crowd, though, the kids all acted as if they hated anything to do with school subjects. They made fun of anyone who was interested in doing anything except fooling around. And Larry knew that when he got to school he'd stand around with the gang instead of going into the library, just because he couldn't bear to have the kids ride him about being a brain.

It was always the same old story. Just like last Sunday—Larry had been on the way to the museum to see a special exhibit about prehistoric animals. On the bus he'd met Pete and Jake, and without even mentioning the museum, he had let them talk him into going to see *The Werewolf Strikes Again*, a movie that he didn't even want to see.

Like the chameleon, Larry always blended in. He just couldn't make himself be different from the crowd, no matter how much he wanted to. It seemed silly that "being yourself" could be so hard.

What should Larry do?

Possible Discussion Topics:

1. Have you ever felt like Larry, finding it difficult to "be yourself?"
2. How can Larry do what he is really interested in and still keep his buddies?
3. Do you think Larry is hurting himself by not being more assertive?

WHAT SHOULD BERNARD DO?

Bernard's been "rescued" by Jack's help with his arithmetic problems but now Jack asks if he can copy Bernard's geography paper.

Social studies he loved. Geography he loved. Science and spelling he loved. But when it came to arithmetic, well, Bernard preferred going to the dentist to working problems. By struggling hard, he had managed to get through multiplication and long division, but when fractions came along, Bernard was way out in space.

And then Jack Cromley came to his rescue. One afternoon when Bernard had gone home with Jack to see his new telescope, Bernard got to talking about how hard fractions were for him. "How come you catch on right away, Jack?" he asked.

"Oh, fractions are simple," Jack said. The boys sat down in the living room and Jack started at the beginning, just the way the teacher had, by drawing a pie and dividing it into pieces. At first, Bernard still didn't understand, but Jack was patient and went over it all again. Finally, the idea got through to Bernard. When he got home, he had no trouble working out that day's problems.

From then on, every time there was an assignment he couldn't figure out, Bernard would go to Jack's house and Jack would explain the work until Bernard could do the problems.

"Jack Cromley has been wonderful to you," Bernard's mother said.

Wonderful isn't the word for it, Bernard thought now as he walked up the school steps. Gosh, I was drowning in the ocean and Jack threw me a life preserver, that's what. My arithmetic grades are better and I've almost started to like arithmetic.

Bernard had just hung up his jacket when Jack came racing down the hall.

"Listen, Bernie," he said, panting, "I didn't get a chance to do that geography assignment last night. My uncle came for a visit. Give me your answers and let me copy them before Mrs. Towers collects the papers."

Bernard stared at Jack. Copying was cheating, and he didn't like the idea at all. But how could he possibly refuse Jack, who had helped him so much? What should Bernard do?

Possible Discussion Topics:

1. Have you ever had to say no to a friend because what they asked seemed wrong to you? Tell about it.
2. When a person truly helps you, are you obligated to do anything they ask of you?
3. Do you worry that if you refuse to do something for a friend, no matter how good your reason, they will stop being your friend?

WHAT SHOULD GUY DO?

Guy is miserable in a new school. He knows he has to spend only a year there but can't figure out how to make the best of it.

Guy hated his new school so much that he didn't have time to like anything any more.

Just one month ago, he was spending the summer in the same house where he'd lived all his life and was planning to start sixth grade in the same school he'd gone to since kindergarten. His friends would all be in his room and he was a cinch to make the baseball team. And then, just before school opened, the family had moved to a little town Guy hadn't even been able to find on the map. As far as Guy was concerned, the world had come to an end.

Guy didn't like their new house or the town or the people. He started to school and the school was so different from the one back home that Guy could hardly stand it.

"Don't be such a poor sport, Guy," his mother said to him one night after he had spent the dinner hour complaining. "We'll only be here a year and then we'll be going back. Make the best of it."

In a year, all the gang at home would have forgotten him, Guy thought. Besides, the school here was probably so poor that he might even have to repeat the sixth grade when he returned. That night he went to sleep trying to pretend that he was back in his old bedroom.

The next day, things seemed worse than ever. What a school, Guy thought. So small that there isn't even a cafeteria, so all morning long you keep smelling what people have in their lunch bags.

Today, the room was unusually stuffy and somebody had brought some kind of cheese that smelled terrible. Even though a light drizzle was falling when the noon bell rang, Guy went outside and hunched up against the schoolhouse wall while he ate his sandwiches.

Looking glumly at the mud puddles on the dreary school yard, he munched away without knowing whether he was eating peanut butter or bologna. He was thinking about what his father had said at breakfast that morning:

"Guy, you're too smart to spend a whole year griping about things that can't be changed. Surely, you can find something else to do besides wasting your time on hating."

Guy wanted to figure out a way to have a good year, but he didn't know how to start. How could he have a good year in this miserable school away from all his friends?

What should Guy do?

Possible Discussion Topics:

1. Do you think Guy was a poor sport?
2. What could Guy do to make his life at the new school more pleasant?
3. What could other pupils at the school do to make his life more pleasant?

WHAT SHOULD GERRI DO?

When her friend Doug talks the teacher into letting Gerri play guitar in the play, she's not pleased. Gerri knows she's not good enough, but Doug says she'll be letting him down if she backs out of the performance.

The fifth graders were putting on a play for the entire school. The director was Doug Harding, Gerri's best friend. He had tried to get a part in the play for Gerri, but Mrs. Solak had put Gerri in charge of publicity instead.

It wasn't the same as being on stage, Gerri thought, but at least she'd get her name on the program. She'd do the best she could on publicity, and maybe she'd get a chance some other time to act.

But Doug believed that best friends were supposed to stick together, so he didn't give up. And one afternoon, as Gerri was walking home from school, Doug came running up full of news.

"It's not exactly a part," he panted, "but I got you the next best thing. Mrs. Solak said she wanted someone to sit on the side of the stage between acts and play the guitar. I told her you'd add a lot to the program, and she said you could do it."

"Me!" said Gerri. "Why, Cliff Nelson is twice as good as I am. He took lessons for two years."

"So what?" said Doug. "I told Mrs. Solak how great you were when you played at the class picnic, and she's real impressed."

"That wasn't anything big—just fooling around," Gerri protested. "I've never even had a lesson."

Doug looked hurt. "Listen, Gerri, I went to a lot of trouble for you, so don't let me down. If you tell Mrs. Solak to get someone else, it'll make me look like a dope after all the bragging I did about you."

"You'll make both of us look like the worst kind of dopes if I try to play and get all fouled up."

Gerri tried to think what to do. She knew she was not good enough to play before the school—and not even half as good as Cliff Nelson. Doug was always exaggerating. But he'd gone out of his way to be helpful, and Gerri hated to let him down.

What should Gerri do?

Possible Discussion Topics:

1. If Gerri embarrasses herself in front of the school by playing the guitar badly, will Doug have done her a favor? Will she have done Doug a favor?
2. How might Gerri arrange for Cliff Nelson to play the guitar without offending Doug?
3. How might Gerri handle Doug's exaggerations in the future?

WHAT SHOULD SAMANTHA DO?

Afraid of spoiling her 100% perfect record on spelling tests, Samantha's tempted to cheat.

Samantha had been sick in bed with a sore throat for three days. On Thursday, when she went back to school, Mr. Jencks gave her several papers and the weekly list of new spelling words.

Samantha stuck them all in her pocket and remembered to give the PTA notice to her mother when she got home from school. Then she sat down with a peanut butter sandwich to study the new words.

Division, magazine, attract, engineer. . . . Talk about hard! Where did Mr. Jencks dig up these words, anyway? How was she supposed to learn them all in one day?

Samantha began copying the words, trying to remember whether *attract* had one *t* or two, whether *engineer* began with an *e* or an *i*. Samantha had made 100 on every spelling test so far, and she didn't want to ruin her record.

Friday morning she was still confused about how to spell several of the words. She had an awful feeling that she would misspell some of them.

It just wasn't fair, she told herself, that everybody else had had four days to study the list while she'd had only one. Suddenly she reached for her ruler. On the back she copied all the words she wasn't sure of.

Now she could get a perfect score. She would keep the ruler on her desk and look at it when she was in doubt about a word. Then she'd study the spelling words hard over the weekend so she'd really earn the 100 she was going to get. That made it fair. But did it? When Mr. Jenks passed out the paper for the spelling test, Samantha was still undecided about whether she should copy the words from the ruler.

What should Samantha do?

Possible Discussion Topics:

1. What should Samantha have done when she realized that she wasn't ready for the test?
2. Is it honest to get a good grade by copying if you study later?
3. Which is most important: for Samantha to learn to spell the words, to get 100, or to be able to figure out the right thing to do?

WHAT SHOULD DONALD DO?

Donald has a conflict—he wants to go to New York when his responsibilities as a caroling manager and singer tell him to stay home.

The week before Christmas was going to be different at Meadow Junior High this year. Instead of the usual parties, the students had planned projects to make Christmas happier for people whose lives were usually pretty dreary. The chorus had promised to do its share by singing carols at the hospitals.

Miss Marchetti, the music teacher, had asked Donald if he would be manager for the caroling expedition, saying she had picked him because he was so levelheaded and reliable. Donald felt proud and agreed to take the job, even after the teacher had explained that it involved lots of work and responsibility.

Besides his duties as manager, Donald was one of the three altos in the chorus, so he was kept really busy, what with rehearsals and taking care of all the advance details of the caroling trip. However, by Wednesday, two days before the performance, Donald had things well organized: the green choir robes were sorted, ready for him to distribute, enough parents had volunteered to provide transportation, and the time schedules were worked out.

When Donald got home from school on Wednesday, he found his Aunt Sally there with his mother.

"Donald, wait until you hear Aunt Sally's surprise," his mother said.

"It's really a Christmas present," said Aunt Sally. Then she went on to explain she and Uncle Arnold and Donald's cousin Fred were going to drive to New York to meet Uncle Arnold's business partner, who was coming home from a trip to Europe.

"Uncle Arnold and I decided this morning that we should take you with us," she said. "You'll enjoy meeting the plane, and afterward you and Fred can go ice-skating at Rockefeller Center Plaza. We'll see the Christmas pageant at Radio City Music Hall and you boys can take a ride through Central Park in a horse-drawn carriage. We plan to leave here early Friday and come back Saturday evening."

"Oh, Mother I *can* go, can't I? We won't be doing much work on the last day before vacation."

Then Donald remembered the caroling on Friday afternoon. There would be lots of last minute details. Still, he told himself, he had done a good deal of work already and maybe he could get Tom to take over. Of course, the alto section would miss him, but maybe it could get by with just two altos.

Donald hated to be a quitter and had often complained about people who were. But he had only been to New York once before, and this was a wonderful chance. Should he do what he had agreed to do or accept Aunt Sally's offer?

What should Donald do?

Possible Discussion Topics:

1. Does Donald have any choices? Can Tom take over for him?
2. Would the other carolers think Donald was a quitter if he went to New York? Would Donald?
3. Should Donald's mother have warned his Aunt about his commitment before she issued the invitation?

WHAT SHOULD MICHAEL DO?

After he tells everyone he is going to play the trumpet solo in the band concert, Michael learns that Sarah will play the solo and that they are to play a duet together.

Michael walked quickly down the school steps, swallowing hard to fight back the tears. He wished Rick would keep still; he certainly wasn't making it any easier.

"Boy, you must feel awful," Rick kept saying. "Everybody was sure you'd get the solo part. Mr. Everett must be crazy to give it to Sarah."

In every band concert for two years, Michael had played a trumpet solo. He could do things with a trumpet that the other kids just wished they could do, and besides, he read music better than anyone else in the band.

When Mr. Everett had told about the plans for the Christmas concert and asked different students to try out for solo parts, Michael knew that there would be a good trumpet part and was certain that he would be the one to play it. He had told his family—even his aunt, uncle, and grandmother—that he would have a solo part, and they had all promised to come to hear him.

Michael had been so sure of his own ability that he didn't even notice how well a new student, Sarah McLean, had played during the tryouts. This afternoon when Mr. Everett had announced that Sarah would play the solo and Michael would appear with Sarah later, in a duet, Michael could hardly believe it.

"I feel like dropping out of the band," he told Rick. "I'd rather not be in the concert at all than have a dumb little part like that."

"That would serve Mr. Everett right," said Rick. "But listen. Nobody else could play that duet with Sarah, so maybe if you say you won't do it, Mr. Everett will have to change his mind and let you play the solo."

Michael left Rick at the corner and walked home slowly, letting his trumpet case bang against his knee. Of course, just because he'd always played solo before didn't mean that Mr. Everett had to let him play one this time. "But," Michael thought to himself, "neither do I have to play that duet!"

Michael couldn't bear to think how embarrassing it would be to have to tell the whole family that he wouldn't be playing the solo. Perhaps if he told Mr. Everett how he'd counted on the part.... What if he told his family he'd persuaded Mr. Everett to give the part to Sarah so that the new student would feel more at home?

What in the world should Michael do?

Possible Discussion Topics:

1. Was it worse for Michael because he lost the solo part to a girl?
2. Should solos or leads always go to the student who is the very best?
3. What can Michael do to make the concert and the duet fun and challenging for himself?

WHAT SHOULD RAMONA DO?

Ramona accidentally ruins a library record. If she pays for it, she won't have money for shoes. But since she forgot to sign it out, need anyone know?

As soon as the last bell rang. Ramona went to the school library to get a phonograph record to take home to the trailer where she and her family lived. She was excited, because being able to borrow records was something new to her. Her family moved from place to place, helping to harvest crops, so she had gone to many schools, but Brookville was the first she'd attended where she could get records.

She selected *Peter and the Wolf*, which she had loved ever since she first heard it in class. She could hardly wait to hear it again. The people in the next trailer owned a record player. She was sure they would let her play the record as soon as they got back from working in the vineyards.

When Ramona was almost to the trailer park, she realized that she had dashed out of the library without signing out the record.

"I'll do it before school tomorrow," she told herself, as she hurried along.

In spite of her haste, she didn't get to hear *Peter and the Wolf*. The shabby red trailer which had been parked next to her family's battered gray one was gone. The grape harvest was nearly over, and the owners of the record player must have started on their way to the next harvest.

Ramona was disappointed. She didn't know anyone else who had a record player, so she wouldn't get to hear the record after all. When she entered her own trailer, not even the good smell of the beans bubbling on the gas plate made her feel any better. She put her books and the record on the shelf over the gas plate and went out to play.

Ramona's parents were always so tired from working in the hot sun all day that everyone went to bed early in the trailer, so Ramona came in soon to get her homework done before supper.

She gasped when she took her school things from the shelf. The steam from the beans had warped the record. It was ruined.

What a stupid thing she had done! Now she remembered the sign on the record rack, "Keep records away from heat." How dumb she had been to forget! She knew the price of *Peter and the Wolf*. To pay for the record would take all of the money she'd earned taking care of the Posey twins every

Saturday for weeks and weeks. And she needed the money to buy new shoes.

And then Ramona remembered that she hadn't signed the record out. Nobody knew she had it. She could throw it away and nobody would ever know what had happened to it.

Would that be stealing? It was her fault that the record was ruined, but didn't she need the new shoes more than the school library needed the record?

Ramona could hardly sleep that night. What should she do?

Possible Discussion Topics:

1. Since she forgot to sign out the record, would Ramona be lying or stealing now by not reporting what happened?
2. Since it was an accident, is it fair for Ramona to pay for the record with money for shoes?
3. Can you think of some ways kids unintentionally steal?

WHAT SHOULD THOMAS DO?

The theme Thomas talked his sister into writing for him is so good that the local newspaper plans to publish it along with the author's—Thomas'—photograph.

"Children, I have some exciting news for you," Miss Jackson announced in social-studies class. "Claudia Brock, the editor of the *Gazette*, heard that you've been studying the history of our town and asked to see the themes you wrote about it.

"She thought they were all so fine that she could hardly believe that they had been written by elementary-school pupils. In fact, she said one of them was so good that she's decided to print it in the paper along with a photograph of the author."

"Whose theme was it?" the children asked excitedly, and then several said, "I'll bet it was Sandra's."

"No," said the teacher, "it wasn't Sandra's, but you're almost right because it was written by her twin brother, Thomas. Congratulations, Thomas. Your mother and father will be really proud when they hear the news, and I'm sure you're thrilled and happy."

Miss Jackson smiled broadly at Thomas but he didn't smile back. He certainly wasn't thrilled and he was far from happy. All day, in fact, he felt as if he'd swallowed a big stone that weighed him down inside.

After the dismissal bell rang, Miss Jackson called him to her desk and said, "Tell Sandra that Ms. Brock had a hard time deciding whether to choose your theme or hers. Please tell her also that I'm sorry she's home sick with a sore throat and hope she'll be back in class soon."

As Thomas walked slowly home, the stony feeling inside him was worse than ever. When he came to his front steps, he didn't run up them as usual. Instead, he sat down to do some hard thinking before he went inside.

As you may have guessed, the reason he felt so bad was because he hadn't written that theme at all. Sandra had written Thomas' theme as well as her own because putting words together was so much easier for her than it was for him. She hadn't wanted to do it, but he had persuaded her that it was all right just this once and had let her copy all of his arithmetic problems in exchange.

What shall I say to Sandra, he thought, and what will Mom and Dad say if I tell them? Oh, what should I do? . . .

Possible Discussion Topics:

1. Would Thomas' predicament be different if he had told the truth right away? Explain.
2. What are some of the possible consequences if Thomas takes credit for the theme?
3. Would Thomas' coercing Sandra to write the theme for him have been less worse if the paper were not going to publish it?

WHAT SHOULD ANNE DO?

Feeling neglected, Anne lies about going on special holidays with her father, including one to Norway. When the class begins to study that country, the teacher asks Anne to tell all she can remember about her recent trip.

She had fibbed so convincingly that Peg and Marlene wholly believed her. She had never dreamed that her tales would get any farther than her two best friends. But now, as she rose shakily to her feet and faced the class, she knew that fibs had a way of getting out of hand.

Anne's parents lived apart. Nine months out of the year, Anne lived with her mother in an apartment on Third Avenue. But when summer came, she always went to her father's farm in Missouri.

The farm was a change from the city, and Anne could swim in the pond there and explore the woods. But her father never had much time to do things or go places with her. When she arrived in Missouri, he and Aunt Beth, his sister, always met her at the train, and they took her to a restaurant for dinner the day she went back to her mother. But in between, one day was like another, with Anne's father hard at work in the fields and Aunt Beth busy around the house.

When summer was over and Anne came back to Third Avenue and her friends' stories of trips to the ocean or Chicago, she longed to have an adventure of her own to tell about.

Then, two years ago, she decided that she couldn't stand just listening any more. She had been reading the travel books in the school library—about California, Canada, Switzerland, and Africa. That year, when she returned from the farm and her friends asked what she had done, she made up a most extraordinary story about a trip out West with her father. She described Yellowstone Park and the Grand Canyon and Disneyland and the Coast just as she had read about them in books. Her story was so lively and vivid that the kids listened wide-eyed. The next year Anne really went overboard and told them that she and her father had gone to Norway.

But now the class began to study Norway, and Marlene put up her hand and said that Anne had actually been there. Miss Ainsworthy said, "Why, Anne, we'd love to hear about your trip! Please tell us all you can remember."

And here Anne was, her heart pounding and her legs numb, staring into her favorite teacher's face. How could she possibly lie to her? What if the children asked questions she couldn't answer. What should Anne do?

Possible Discussion Topics:

1. Somehow Anne feels cheated, although many children do not get to travel as much as she does. Is there anything about her situation which might make her feel she needs something special?
2. Is it ever a good policy to make someone think you are something other than what you are? Is it fair to yourself?
3. What does Anne think might happen if she told the girls the truth? What might really happen?

WHAT SHOULD MARCIE DO?

Pride prevents Marcie from accepting free school lunches; by mid-afternoon she is so hungry she can't concentrate.

By two o'clock every afternoon, Marcie was so hungry that all she could think of was the lunch she would have had if she had eaten in the school cafeteria—a hamburger or spaghetti with meatballs or even fried chicken, and dessert and milk, too. The trouble was that Marcie had free lunch tickets this year and she hated to go to the cafeteria and hand the cashier a ticket instead of paying for her lunch with money the way she had done until a few weeks ago.

Marcie had asked her mother to let her carry lunch to school. "I could fix it myself, Mother—a hard-boiled egg and a sandwich."

"I don't have a penny to spare these days," her mother replied. "Those lunch tickets are meant for people like us who are having a tough time. It would be like throwing money away not to use them." Marcie didn't admit that the free tickets embarrassed her. She knew that her mother would say, "Who's going to know or care about something like that!"

Marcie realized that she couldn't keep on as she was. She was so hungry in the afternoon that she couldn't concentrate on geography and arithmetic. Twice, the teacher had asked her if she felt sick. She had answered no. What really makes me feel sick, she thought, is the idea of having anyone in school see me using the free tickets. Marcie had never actually heard anybody say anything about the children who received free lunches, but she imagined that the other kids looked at them rather pityingly.

Marcie hated being hungry, but she couldn't bear the thought of being pitied. What should Marcie do?

Possible Discussion Topics:

1. Before Marcie had the tickets, do you suppose she thought people looked pityingly at children who did?
2. Is it possible that, although money is a problem in Marcie's family, other families have worse problems?
3. Can you think of some lasting problems that might arise if Marcie continues to refuse to eat a nourishing lunch?

WHAT SHOULD DONNA DO?

Donna accidentally finds out Kathy's father is in jail and tells Janice and some of the other kids. They laugh at Kathy and make her cry. Donna decides she wants to do something to to make up for what she did.

When Donna was going out the school door for recess, some of her jacks and her ball fell behind the shrubbery under the office window. While she was scrabbling around for them, she heard her teacher, Miss Redmond, talking to the principal.

"Kathy broke down and told me," Miss Redmond was saying, "that the reason she was out last week was that she and her mother went out of town to visit her father in jail."

"I really admire Kathy for telling you about it," the principal said. "What a tragic situation!"

Donna stuffed the ball and jacks into her pocket and ran over to where Janice was waiting for her.

"Janice," she yelled, "I've got something to tell you!"

As Donna was telling Janice what she had overheard, some of the other third graders joined them and Donna let them in on what she had learned. Before long, most of the class knew why Kathy had been absent.

When the bell rang and the children lined up to go in, Kathy was right behind Janice. Janice smiled a mean smile and said:

"How's your father, Kathy? I heard you visited him last week."

One or two of the kids snickered. Kathy flushed a deep pink.

Donna sat uncomfortably through reading and science, her eyes on Kathy. Kathy hardly moved. She didn't open her workbook. She didn't write her spelling words. She just sat and stared out the window. Finally, she put her head down on her desk and simply sobbed. When Miss Redmond went to her and asked what was the trouble, Kathy choked out:

"You told. You told. All the kids know and they're all laughing."

Donna felt terrible. She had been so pleased with herself for knowing something she wasn't supposed to know that she couldn't resist the temptation to tell the others. The idea that Kathy might find out that everybody knew about her father had never entered Donna's head. Maybe she could do something now to make up for what she had done. But what? What should Donna do?

Possible Discussion Topics:

1. Why was the teasing particularly unfair to Kathy? Is teasing ever fair?
2. When someone learns a secret by accident, do they have any obligation to keep it?
3. If Donna told the secret but made the kids promise not to let Kathy know they heard it, would she be to blame if someone broke the promise?

WHAT SHOULD JIMMY DO?

After a day of rebellious behavior, of "being his own boss," Jimmy wonders if keeping it up won't take considerable effort and let him in for a lot of trouble.

Jimmy woke up one day and decided he wasn't going to say "Good morning" or "Hi" to anybody. He told himself that he was absolutely sick of saying the same old things and doing the same old things that everybody else said and did. He wanted to be different. And this meant, first of all, that he wasn't going to go around opening his mouth like a dumb goldfish all day, saying "Hi" and "How-are-you?"

When he was dressing, he decided to leave his belt off his pants. He hated belts and from now on, he decided, he wouldn't wear one. When his mother asked him at breakfast why he was putting peanut butter on his toast, he said it was because he felt like it. And when he passed old Mrs. Summers on his way to school and she said, "Hello, Jimmy, how are you?" he said, "Pretty bad."

At school, he went up the front stairs instead of the side ones even though he knew the front was reserved for the younger children, because he couldn't think of a good reason why he shouldn't.

He wrote his spelling test in red pencil instead of black because he liked red better, even though Miss King frowned about it. He spent recess digging for Indian arrowheads at the back of the schoolyard instead of playing the usual game of volleyball. And when he left for home at three o'clock in a downpour, he refused to wear his raincoat.

And while he sloshed through the puddles, the rain running down his neck, he made up his mind that he would definitely not do the paper on insects that Miss King had assigned. Ever since first grade they had been learning about the usefulness of bugs, and he was absolutely not going to do it any more. He had a lot more important things to do with his time.

It felt good for a change to be his own boss and discover the real Jimmy beneath all those layers of "Good morning" and "How-are-you?" And yet, something told him that he might be letting himself in for a lot of trouble. And something else told him it was going to take a lot of effort just to be different. Still, he didn't want to go through life being nothing but a colorless blob of oatmeal, did he—a mere doorknob, a baked potato? What should Jimmy do?

Possible Discussion Topics:

1. Was Jimmy deliberately trying to make trouble, or did he have a good point in being impatient with the same old things?
2. How can you decide which things are worth making an issue of and which are not?
3. Should a person be different by *trying* to be, or should he just be himself and let his natural differences show up automatically?

WHAT SHOULD CLYDE DO?

Clyde decides to become a loner because he cries so easily and is teased so much for it.

It was a big problem, and it seemed to be getting worse. Mother said it was all in his mind. Dad said it was physiological, whatever that meant. Grandmother said he wasn't getting enough sleep. The kids said he was a great big crybaby—period. The fact was that every time something didn't go just right—if somebody tripped him or beat him at checkers—Clyde started to cry.

He fought against it, but even though he bit his lips and squeezed his eyes shut, his mouth would tremble and the fat tears would begin sliding down his cheeks. Then the other kids would jeer and the whole ocean would come gushing out. It made Clyde hate himself and everybody else. How many times had he heard somebody say that boys weren't supposed to cry?

"Clyde, Clyde, run and hide," they yelled, or "Crybaby, Clyde-baby, do you want your mama, maybe?" Clyde would be so furious he would lash out blindly with his fists, and once he got sent to the principal.

Last Thursday was the worst. Clyde was giving his book report in front of the room and had meant to say, "building the boat," but said, "boading the bilt," instead. Instantly the room was filled with laughter. Clyde stopped. He felt the blood rushing to his face. He tried to go on, but he felt his lips tremble, his eyes cloud, and the next moment he was bawling in front of the whole class.

"That's okay, Clyde," said Mr. Jackson. "When you feel ready, go right on. We all make mistakes, and that was really just a funny one, wasn't it?"

But it wasn't funny to Clyde. As he walked home that afternoon, he made up his mind. Unless he had to, he wasn't going to do anything or go anyplace or talk to anyone, ever again. He was through with being embarrassed. He'd stay in his room and fool with his trains and watch television, and it would be Clyde the Loner from now on. He knew it wouldn't make him happy, but it would be better than going on like this. Or would it be better? What should Clyde do?

Possible Discussion Topics:

1. Do you think Clyde's classmates would behave any differently if he didn't get so angry when teased?
2. Is it all right for girls and boys and even grownups to cry sometimes? Why or why not?
3. Do you think Clyde's plan for crying less was a good one?

WHAT SHOULD STEPHANIE DO?

When no one is watching, Stephanie pockets a piece of school property she desperately wants and then tries to think of reasons to keep it.

It was the only thing Stephanie had ever stolen in her life, and she did it so quickly she hardly had time to think about it.

Her class had been studying relics of the American past, and the school's collection of Indian arrowheads was on display in the room. Every day Stephanie stood before the arrowheads, thrilled to her fingertips as she thought of how, hundreds of years ago, real Indians had actually held these arrowheads in their hands. Perhaps they had been used to bring down buffalo or deer. Stephanie wished that she owned an arrowhead to keep in her room and to hold in her hand while she imagined what it was like centuries ago in this country.

One morning while the students were milling around in the classroom before the bell, she noticed that one of the arrowheads was lying on the floor beneath the exhibit table. She stooped to pick it up, and suddenly, realizing that no one was watching her, she slipped it in her pocket instead of putting it on the table and went back to her seat.

Her heart pounding, she looked around, but no one was paying any attention to her. She was safe. Even if Mr. Dyron discovered that the arrowhead was missing, he certainly would not search everybody. Anyway, there were 11 arrowheads left; it wasn't as though she had taken them all.

She opened her book as the bell rang, but instead of reading, she began thinking of reasons that justified what she had done. The school owed her something, she told herself. Just think of all the things she had lost here. There was the time she put a dime in the candy machine in the basement and nothing came out. And what about the pencil she'd loaned Mr. Dyron that he'd never returned? What about the quarter that she'd lost somewhere on the playground? What about the time the teacher got the milk orders mixed up and gave her plain old white instead of chocolate?

When you added it up, it probably came to a lot more than an old Indian arrowhead was worth. She was just getting something back for all the things the school owed her, that's all.

Stephanie's heart continued to pound, though, and the arrowhead in her pocket felt more like a big boulder weighing her down. There was still plenty of time to return it, and probably no one would see her do it. But she had got it this far and was reluctant to give it back. Wasn't it really hers, in fair exchange for the other things the school owed her? Or was it? What should Stephanie do?

Possible Discussion Topics:

1. Do Stephanie's "reasons" for keeping the arrowhead hold up?
2. Why does Stephanie need such excuses?
3. Can dishonesty become a habit?

WHAT SHOULD MARIA DO?

Maria's job at school was cleaning out the supply cupboard. She loved art and would take home the broken throw-away crayons. But they became bigger and bigger . . . and sometimes she took some unmarked drawing paper.

Next to Christmas and birthdays, Maria liked drawing and painting more than anything else in the world. She liked to draw sleek brown horses with white spots on their legs. She liked to paint pictures of tulips and robins. And she spent many hours drawing girls in long, glittering dresses.

"Maria is a real little artist," her mother said one evening. "I wish we had money to buy her all the paints and paper and crayons she needs."

Maria's father sighed. With seven other children in the family, there were more important things to buy, such as shoes and caps and sweaters.

At school, Maria's teacher gave her the job of cleaning out the supply cupboard. Every Friday, Maria stayed after school to sort out the crayons, put the paints and chalk away, stack the drawing paper, and sharpen the pencils.

Sometimes the teacher would come by and say, "Oh, that paint is all dried up. Better throw that jar out, Maria." Or "Why don't you throw away all the little stubs of crayons? The children don't use them."

But short, broken pieces were better than no crayons at all, so Maria always took them home instead of throwing them out. All week long she would look forward to Friday. She wondered how many pieces she'd find, or how many sheets of drawing paper had marks on them, or how many jars of paint might be drying up. Always, instead of throwing these things out, Maria slipped them in her lunch box and took them home.

Before long Maria was taking home bigger and bigger pieces of crayon. Sometimes she took a few sheets of drawing paper that weren't marked up at all or a jar of paint that was still quite soft. Every week it was harder and harder for her to decide what was good enough to leave in the cupboard and what she should take home.

One day the teacher said, "My goodness! What happened to the magenta crayon? I was sure we had one here." And Maria remembered that she had taken it home because it had broken in two.

Maria began to feel very uncomfortable. She was not sure what was right and what was wrong. Nobody else knew what she had been doing. Maybe she should stop taking anything. But it did seem foolish to throw out useful materials. What should Maria do?

Possible Discussion Topics:

1. Have you ever felt like Maria, not knowing where right became wrong?
2. If Maria had talked to the teacher about the throw-aways, might it have helped her know what to do?
3. Do you think Maria is stealing?

WHAT SHOULD NICOLAS DO?

Nicolas doesn't want to be a tattletale but the broken lock on the side door is serious and he thinks it ought to be reported to the janitor.

Before school, Don led Nicolas around the building to the side door—the one that was always locked. Two other kids he knew were there, acting as though something very mysterious were going on.

"What's up?" Nicolas asked.

"Shhh, look!" Don Bradford reached out to the door knob, turned it, and the door opened. "See, the lock is broken. Wouldn't the principal have fits knowing this?"

"We discovered it yesterday and came over last night," confided one of the boys. "Golly, did we have fun! We went through every room in the school, and Don even sat in the principal's chair. Was he a riot!"

Nicolas laughed as he imagined Don, with his wild red hair and his bright green shirt, sitting pompously at the desk where the gray-haired, gray-suited principal usually sat. But then he said, "Gee, shouldn't someone tell the janitor about the broken lock? Somebody else might get in and take things."

Don frowned. "You going to tattle? What do you think we'll do, burn the place down?"

"No, I don't suppose you guys would do any harm, but what if somebody else found out about it—robbers, maybe, or even escaped prisoners."

"No one's going to find out about it unless you go squealing and spoil everything," Don said. "I wish we'd never told you." Don turned his back to the door and started to whistle nonchalantly as a couple of teachers came around the building.

In geography class, Nicolas stared at the map of Australia without really seeing it. Nobody had ever thought he was a tattletale before, and he had often felt disgusted with kids who went running to the teachers about everything instead of working out problems for themselves.

Somehow this seemed different, though. There wasn't anything Nicolas could do about it by himself. Don and the others probably wouldn't destroy school property on purpose while they were inside, but what if they fooled with something like a projector and had an accident? Or what if somebody bad from outside the school got in through the side door?

Nicolas saw the teacher looking at him and went back to studying the map, but he couldn't keep his mind on it. The janitor was bound to discover the broken lock and get a new one, so why worry? Yet if something were broken or stolen, Nicolas would feel guilty because he hadn't told anyone. He didn't want to get the other fellows in trouble or spoil their fun—he didn't want to be a squealer—but he didn't want to keep on worrying, either. What *should* Nicolas do?

Possible Discussion Topics:

1. Is there a difference between being a tattletale and reporting something serious that might cause personal injury or property damage?
2. Have you ever "squealed" and been glad you did? Why?
3. Will Nicolas lose Don as a friend if he tells?

WHAT SHOULD LANIE DO?

James constantly borrows things from Lanie. Today it was her eraser and because of it, Lanie didn't finish the last row of problems on her test.

Lanie wanted desperately to finish the last row of problems before Mrs. King asked for the papers, but James kept jabbing her in the back with a lead pencil, and she had to turn around.

"Let me borrow your eraser," James whispered. "I've got to erase a whole row."

"I might need it myself," Lanie told him.

"Aw c'mon, I'll give it right back."

Arguing with James was taking more time than letting him borrow the eraser, so Lanie passed it behind her and went on with her problems.

But she was angry, and instead of thinking about long division, all she could think about was how she'd like to punch James in the nose the next time he bothered her during a test. A hundred times a week, it seemed, James had to borrow something—a pen, paper, scissors, ruler.

"Two more minutes to go," said Mrs. King, softly.

Lanie hurriedly wrote down the next problem and then realized she was doing it wrong. She reached for her eraser and then remembered James had it. She turned around. "Where's my eraser?" she whispered.

But James was working feverishly to finish the problems on time, and only pointed to the floor where the eraser had fallen under the desk behind him. Lanie had to get up and walk clear around the row to get it. She was furious now, and bore down so heavily on her pencil that she broke the lead and had to go to the pencil sharpener. She had just taken her seat again when she heard Mrs. King saying, "Time's up. Lay down your pencils and pass in your papers."

Lanie was terribly upset. She had to do something about James's borrowing. What should she do?

Possible Discussion Topics:

1. Why did Lanie put up with James' borrowing for so long?
2. What are some ways you can let your friends know how you feel about things like borrowing?
3. What are some of the consequences of getting angry inside instead of talking things over with friends?

WHAT SHOULD DOUG DO?

Doug has an opportunity, but is afraid to tell about his trouble with the neighborhood bully.

Doug left home ten minutes early so that he could walk to school the long way instead of cutting across the big parking lot. Three times this week Walter and Tony, sixth graders, had jumped on him from behind a parked car, taken his lunch money, and threatened to beat him up if he told anybody. If they were waiting for him again this morning, Doug thought, perhaps he could fool them by starting early and taking a different route.

When Doug got as far as the Acme Drugstore, he felt safe. He was looking at some model cars in the window of the closed store when he heard Tony's voice. "Hi, Little Moneybags." The plan hadn't worked. Tony was alone, though. Doug thought that since it wouldn't be two against one this time, he might have a fighting chance. He tried to hit Tony, but the big boy grabbed both his arms and kicked him in the shins.

Just then a police cruiser pulled to the curb beside the boys and a policeman got out. "Hey, you guys. What's going on here?" he asked.

Doug was petrified. He wished that he could simply hand over his lunch money to Tony and run. Just last month, his big brother had been in trouble with the police for driving a friend's motorcycle without a license. Now maybe this policeman would arrest him too.

Tony answered the policeman. "I'm just showing Doug a wrestling hold."

"Well, take it easy," the officer said. "You'd both better get along to school."

Tony patted Doug on the back. "Come on, kid. I'll race you to the corner."

Doug knew that once they were around the corner, Tony would take his lunch money and Doug would be lucky not to have his arm twisted or his thumbs bent back.

He wondered what would happen if he told the officer the true story. What if the policeman said, the way his mother always did, "It takes two to make trouble," and took them both to the station house? Doug hated to think of going without lunch again, but his mother had told him that if *he* ever got into trouble with the police, he'd be in even more trouble at home. What should Doug do?

Possible Discussion Topics:
1. Do you think the policeman might have arrested Doug?
2. What might have happened if Doug had told the policeman the truth?
3. Would you have been afraid to ask the policeman for help?

WHAT SHOULD MOLLY DO?

Molly and other younger kids are being harassed on the way to school by a gang of toughs who demand their lunch money and threaten them. No one dares to tell about it.

The gang hadn't been too much of a problem when Molly was in first and second grade because her older brother had been around to protect her. But now that Wally was in junior high and Molly walked to school alone, they were making her life miserable.

Halfway to the school she'd meet up with them. If she was lucky, they'd be kidding around with each other and she could get by unnoticed, or maybe the patrol guard at the corner would have an eye on them. But if she wasn't lucky, and she usually wasn't, they'd grab her arm as she went by.

"Lend us your lunch money," they'd say, and it didn't make any difference if she said yes or no. They took it anyway, and she never got it back.

And then, all the way to school they'd walk right behind her and talk about the horrible things that would happen if she ever told on them. They'd slash her bike tires or kidnap her dog or do something even worse.

So Molly would go without lunch and say she wasn't hungry. Others in her class said they weren't hungry and skipped lunch too, so Molly knew she wasn't the gang's only victim. But nobody ever complained. It was something they all were aware of but no one ever dared to talk about it.

Molly tried all sorts of things. She'd beg her mother to pack her a lunch instead of giving her money, and sometimes she would. Even when she carried her lunch, however, her mother occasionally gave her money and asked her to pick up something at the grocery store on her way home. If the gang nabbed her on one of those days, she'd have to think up a story to tell her mother.

Molly was really afraid to go to school. Once, when she took her lunch, an older kid pushed her hard just because she didn't have any money. That was the time Molly came closest to telling her brother what was going on, but thinking about what dreadful things the gang might do stopped her. What should Molly do?

Possible Discussion Topics:

1. Since more students than just Molly are bullied, what might they be able to do about it as a group?
2. Why do some people become bullies?
3. Would Molly be wiser to tell her brother or the school principal about this situation? Why?

WHAT SHOULD BILL DO?

Bill is being picked on by a bully. His friends are no help, and even his dad thinks he should learn to fight back.

Something would have to happen soon, because otherwise Bill would just stop going to school. He'd get a stomachache or cut his finger or break a leg or throw up—anything to escape Jim Corley and his bullying.

He realized that the way he acted when Jim teased him only made things worse. He realized that every time he took a new route home from school, Jim knew why and picked on him even more about that. He realized that he was losing friends because he was afraid to stand up to Jim Corley.

Sometimes the boys called Bill a sissy. Sometimes they told him to grow up. But most of the time, they would just say to Jim, "Oh, leave him alone," and give Bill a disgusted look. But this didn't stop Jim from bullying and didn't stop Bill from being scared, so the situation kept getting worse.

It all began one day when Jim was teasing him about something and Bill practically started crying. That was the mistake. He'd thought about it later and wished he'd done *anything* that day except get so upset. Then it would have blown over, and Jim would have left him alone. Instead, it got worse each day.

It never happened at school—always on the way home. Jim would trip him or sock him in the shoulder or grab his cap or knock the books out of his arms or block the sidewalk and not let him pass. Jim was a bully, and he showed no sign at all of changing.

Once Bill complained to the teacher about it, and she warned Jim to stop. But the next week Jim was picking on him worse than ever, and Bill's friends acted as though he shouldn't have told on Jim.

"I'll put a stop to it!" Bill's mother said. "Just tell me the next time it happens, and I'll go see the principal!"

But Bill stopped talking to her about it. The boys would really hate him if the principal got involved.

"What Jim needs is a good punch in the jaw," said Bill's father. "Why don't you learn to defend yourself? Then you won't have any more trouble."

But Bill knew he couldn't be much of a fighter, and Jim was tough. There had to be some other way to handle the problem, but what? What should Bill do?

Possible Discussion Topics:

1. What makes a boy behave like Jim Corley?
2. Is fighting the best way to handle a situation like this?
3. What else might Bill do? How might he get the help of his friends?

WHAT SHOULD LISA AND NANCY DO?

A black girl and a white girl find themselves at odds with their classmates when they refuse to take sides in a silly squabble that has divided blacks and whites.

It all started with an argument between two girls, each of whom insisted she should be first in the lunch line. Betty, a white girl, and Pearl, a black girl, exchanged angry words. The squabble simmered all day and continued the next morning.

Most of the white students in the class sided with Betty; most of the black students, with Pearl.

Two girls, however, refused to take sides. Lisa, a black girl, and

Nancy, a white girl, argued that Betty and Pearl were both wrong for making an issue over a trivial matter. Lisa suggested the two might flip a coin to decide who should be first in the lunch line.

But other members of the class refused to go along with this suggestion. Instead, they tore into Nancy and Lisa, accusing them of being wishy-washy.

"You should stick up for your race no matter what!" a black girl shouted at Lisa. "What's the matter with you?"

"We won't play with you anymore if you don't take Betty's side," a white girl told Nancy.

Nancy managed to smile at this remark and answered, "OK, don't play with me. But I'm not going to take sides in such a silly argument."

"Neither am I," said Lisa.

Although Both Nancy and Lisa were sure they were right to keep out of the squabble, they could see that thair classmates were now angrier at them than they'd been at either Betty or Pearl. Both Nancy and Lisa realized they'd have some difficult days at school before their classmates forgot about the incident. Meanwhile, what should Lisa and Nancy do?

Possible Discussion Topics:

1. Do you think Lisa and Nancy should have avoided trouble by taking sides as the rest of their classmates did?
2. Does the argument "you should stick up for your race no matter what" make any sense? Explain.
3. Do most fights start over something "silly" that could be settled quickly?

WHAT SHOULD RAY DO?

Everyone's fed up with Chris's bragging and Ray tells the gang it's time to call his bluff. But when the chance comes, Ray realizes the situation is too dangerous.

Ray didn't know what to do about Chris. Neither did anyone else. The one thing they didn't want to do was listen to him. Chris was always bragging. No matter what someone had done, Chris had always done something better. No matter what a kid had found or seen or eaten, Chris had always found or seen or eaten something even bigger. It had reached the point where nobody wanted him around.

Of course, Ray didn't really have to do anything about Chris. It wasn't his problem. But when Chris had moved into his neighborhood, Ray had taken him around and introduced him to all the gang, so he felt sort of responsible.

Once they were talking about surfing.

"Huh! You ought to see me!" said Chris.

"Oh, come off it," somebody said. "You've never even been near the ocean! You wouldn't know a surfboard from a closet door."

"I would too!" said Chris angrily. "Once I rode in on a 10-foot wave without spilling!"

The kids jeered and Chris stormed out.

"You know," said Ray disgustedly, "one of these days we ought to call his bluff. Too bad there isn't an ocean around here."

Later, Ray was sorry he'd ever suggested calling Chris's bluff. After school the next day, some from the class were playing on the monkey bars in the school yard. Chris stood watching them.

"Hah," he scoffed. "I wouldn't waste my time climbing on those measly bars. I can climb a 100-foot tree."

"Let's call his bluff," Janey said to Ray. To Chris she said, "Okay, let's see you do it. Climb that tree right out behind the school."

"Make him go clear to the top," Oscar said gleefully.

"I'll bet he won't even get to the third branch," said another kid.

Oh, yes, he will, Ray thought. Chris was just crazy enough to try it. Ray looked up at the tree. It was tall—and dangerous. Chris didn't even have a decent pair of climbing shoes. If he fell, he might kill himself. It was time to call his bluff, all right, but this was hardly the way to do it:

What should Ray do?

Possible Discussion Topics:

1. Why do some people brag about themselves and even boast about things they can't really do?
2. How could the kids call Chris's bluff without endangering him?
3. What does Chris really need? Do Ray and the others have any responsibility to help him?

WHAT SHOULD GABRIELLE DO?

Gabrielle and James cheat on a make-up test. At the last moment, Gabrielle tears hers up and confesses. James is furious because now the teacher will suspect him.

James and Gabrielle looked at the dittoed sheets Miss Robinson had handed them before the buzzer called her to the office. They had both been out of school the week before with the flu. On Monday, their first day back, Miss Robinson had told them that they had missed an arithmetic test and a grammar test while they were absent and that they would have to take make-up tests after school on Wednesday and Friday—arithmetic on Wednesday, she said, and grammar rules on Friday.

Now it was after school on Wednesday, and James and Gabrielle were alone with the first test.

Suddenly James gasped, "Look, Gabrielle, this is a grammar test! She said it would be arithmetic today."

"I know she did. I can't answer half of these crazy questions."

"It's a dirty trick," James groaned.

"I'll be lucky to get a D on this," Gabrielle said. "This means I'll miss out on the dollar my grandmother sends me when I get an A."

The children worked for a while. Then James said, "I've got the grammar book. Let's use it."

"Do you mean cheat?" said Gabrielle.

"Well, it isn't really cheating, because she said we wouldn't have this grammar test for two days."

Gabrielle knew that James was wrong, and her hand shook, but she copied the answers from the text, right along with him.

When they heard Miss Robinson coming down the hall, James flicked the book closed.

"Lay your papers on my desk," the teacher said. James turned his in and stood waiting for Gabrielle.

"Just one minute more," begged Gabrielle. She looked at her answers, all right answers, she knew. But there were no two ways about it—copying was cheating. If her grandmother sent her a dollar for an A she got by cheating, it would be just plain stealing to take it.

Instead of putting her test on top of James's, Gabrielle tore it up and dropped the pieces in the wastebasket. "Miss Robinson, I'll have to take an F.

I cheated."

Miss Robinson said nothing. Gabrielle left the room and James followed her. As soon as the door was closed, James really lit into Gabrielle. He said that Miss Robinson was bound to be suspicious of his answers because of what Gabrielle had done. He told her that he would tell the other kids Gabrielle was just a scarey baby, and not to have anything to do with her.

Gabrielle worried all night. She knew that the other children always paid a lot of attention to what James wanted. Should she try to tell them her side of the story? Should she talk it over with the teacher? Would the best thing be just to keep quiet?

What should Gabrielle do?

Possible Discussion Topics:

1. What do you think of Gabrielle for confessing? What would you think of her if she had refused to look in the book?
2. Why do you think kids doing something wrong sometimes try to pull someone else in with them?
3. Would you, if you were Gabrielle, talk it over with the teacher or just keep quiet?

WHAT SHOULD SCOTT'S CLASS DO?

Scott's classmates wonder how to deal with this prejudiced snob whose rudeness to minority group children embarrasses them.

The problem was Scott Douglas Miller—age 10, blond hair, gray eyes, white skin. He was a fairly good student, a wonderful basketball player, and he was honest and helpful around the classroom. But he was a big problem to his classmates.

If your name was Thompson or Turner, Scott treated you like a million dollars. If you lived on Sycamore Avenue or Abingdon Drive, he was your best friend. If your skin was white, he'd do anything in the world for you. But if your name was Lopez or Tolero, or if you lived on Second Street, or if your skin was brown or your eyes were slanted, Scott acted as if he didn't know you were around.

At first, nobody realized that Scott was going to be a problem. Then a boy from Mexico joined the class and later, a boy from Italy. And later still, a black girl became a member of the class.

Chico and Tony and Jessie were no better or worse than anybody else. There were a lot of things they could do, a lot of things they couldn't, and if you added up all their good points and all their bad, they came out about even with everybody else's. As far as the other students were concerned, Chico and Tony and Jessie were as much a part of the fifth grade as the other boys and girls were—as much a part as the American flag. But Scott didn't think so.

Sometimes it seemed that he went out of his way to be mean. If Tony asked him a question, Scott would ignore him. If Chico sat down next to him, he'd move his chair somewhere else. And he never chose Jessie when he was a team leader at recess.

It got to be embarrassing, not only to Chico and Tony and Jessie but to the rest of the class as well. It almost seemed as though he *wanted* somebody to look down on and be rude to.

"The way Scott acts just spoils everything," Katherine said one day at lunch. "He's so mean to Chico and Tony and Jessie that it makes me feel sort of sick when I see him. You've probably noticed that he's careful not to let Miss Richards see him acting that way."

"Yes," Paul agreed. "When she has her eye on him, he acts OK. But he won't even sit at the same table with the rest of us in the cafeteria if Tony and Chico are there."

Ginny broke into the conversation. "Let's not just sit around and talk about it. Let's think of some way we can convince Scott that people can be just as good as he is even if they do look or act different. They can certainly be more fun than he is!"

"Is there anything we could say that would make any difference with Scott?" Jack asked.

"Maybe he'd just tell us to mind our own business," said Paul.

"Besides, instead of talking to him I think we ought to do something," Ginny said. "Does anybody have a good idea?"

What do you think the class should do?

Possible Discussion Topics:

1. What are some of the ways children can contribute to the life of the school because they *are* different?
2. In the long run, who do you think Scott is really hurting? Why?
3. Who are some of the people in their school or community the kids in Scott's class might go to for help?

WHAT SHOULD MOIRA DO?

Moira tries to be a fair team captain but Sam, who is spoiled, selfish and the best player, always threatens to quit when he doesn't get his way.

Well, you can't win them all, sighed Moira, the captain of the Wildcats, as the final batter struck out. The series score was tied now, but the fifth-grade Wildcats could still win the series against the sixth-grade Sluggers.

At that moment, over walked Moira's Problem Number One—a two-legged problem in a brown-checked shirt—a problem named Sam.

"Hey, Moira, I thought I was going to get the new glove in this game," said Sam, scowling. "How come you gave it to Pete?"

"He asked for it first," Moira told him. "You can have it next time."

"I'd better, or I'm not going to be on the team," Sam grumbled.

Moira walked away and held her temper. Sam always made the same threat whenever he didn't get his way. And the trouble was that he was the best player on the team and he knew it. He didn't seem to care that he was the worst when it came to popularity.

"I get first bat," Sam said at practice the next afternoon.

"Oh Sam, you always want to be first," Delia said. "Give someone else a chance."

"I'm first bat or I'll...."

"Quit the team," chorused the others. They knew that song by heart.

Sam didn't ask for any favors for a few days and Moira thought that her troubles were over. Then she met Sam on the stairs after school.

"I hear we get our picture in the paper," Sam said.

"Not everybody," Moira told him. "Just one member from each team, with their hands on the bat. George is going to be the guy from ours."

"How come?" Sam's voice had a babyish whine when he was angry. "I'm the best player! How come I don't get to be in it?"

"Coach Mapes said it was up to me, as captain, to say who'd be in the picture, so I put all the names in a box and drew one. George was the lucky one, and I've already told him."

"Well, I'm the best player and you should have picked me. Tell George you've changed your mind or I'm quitting right now. I mean it."

Moira just stared at Sam. It was all so childish. But there wasn't anybody else in the fifth grade to take Sam's place if he quit, and this time he sounded as if he meant it. What should Moira do?

Possible Discussion Topics:

1. What are the responsibilities of a team captain?
2. In what ways can the others help Sam be a better team player?
3. Does Moira think winning is more important than being fair? Do you?

WHAT SHOULD ALAN DO?

Alan wonders how he can be friends with Zoe, or any other girl, without having to put up with a lot of silly teasing from the kids.

As Alan and Zoe turned the corner, they heard shrieks of laughter. Three boys and two girls from their fourth grade class were standing in the entrance to the drugstore. As soon as Alan saw them, he knew what would happen next. Sure enough, all five of them began to chant:

"Alan and Zoe, sitting in a tree, K-I-S-S-I-N-G."

Zoe's face turned a little pink, but she laughed. Alan didn't laugh. He was mad. This was the third time that he and Zoe had been kidded for being together. The first time, Alan had acted as if he hadn't heard them. The second time, he'd told them to cut it out. Wasn't there *anything* he could do to make them quit?

Zoe turned in at the supermarket to buy a loaf of bread for her mother. Still laughing, she said goodbye to Alan and waved to the gang. That didn't get Alan off the hook, though. The other children, still chanting their silly rhyme, started to march in time with it, and followed Alan down the street.

Then Conrad called, "Hey, Alan, did you kiss her?"

"They were holding hands at recess," Pam said.

Alan scowled. She was making that up. It was all a lot of nonsense, anyhow. He and Zoe just happened to live next door to each other. Both of them were raising guppies, so they had lots to talk about. Zoe was smart, could throw a ball with terrific speed, and could draw better than anyone he knew. He liked the horses she drew; they almost came alive on the paper.

But here in this school if a boy and a girl were friends, everyone thought they were "going steady." All you had to do was hand a girl a pencil or talk with her on the way home from school and the whole class teased you for a week. It didn't seem to bother the girls much, judging from the way Zoe was acting, but Alan was disgusted. He wanted to find some way he could be friends with Zoe or any other girl without having to put up with all the teasing. He never wanted to hear that stupid chant again.

What should Alan do?

Possible Discussion Topics:

1. Can a boy and girl be friends in your class without others teasing them?
2. Think back to the first time you thought it was wrong or silly or no fun to play with the boys/girls in your class, did you question your feelings? Were they right, wrong, or just what everybody did?
3. Are different things expected of girls and boys in your school? What kinds of things?

WHAT SHOULD SHERRY DO?

Burdened with helping her working mother with household chores and the younger children, Sherry is too exhausted to do her homework.

Sherry could hardly keep from crying in front of the whole class when the teacher bawled her out for coming to school without her homework three days in a row. She wondered what the teacher would say if she told her she wouldn't be able to do her homework anymore, ever. Since her father had gone away and Mom had gone to work, Sherry was so busy with jobs around home that she just didn't have time for anything else.

As soon as Sherry got home from school in the afternoon, she had to get her baby brother from the lady across the hall and take care of him until Mom got home from her job at the dry cleaning plant. At four-thirty, she had to wrap the baby in a blanket and take him with her while she went to the day-care center to get Gwen and Bobby. The next hour, until her mother got home, was like a bad dream, with Sherry trying to keep Gwen and Bobby from throwing things at each other or being too rough with the baby.

Mom would flop into a chair and kick her shoes off the minute she got home. While her mother watched the kids, Sherry had to go out to do the day's marketing. Because the little stores in their neighborhood charged much more than the big market on 97th Street, Sherry had to walk clear over there, and sometimes the checkout lines would be long. Often, it would be half-past six before Sherry got home with the groceries.

Mom cooked dinner while Sherry gave the baby his bottle and put him to bed. After dinner, Sherry cleared the table, washed the dishes, and cleaned up the kitchen.

By nine o'clock, when her chores were done and the kids had quieted down, Sherry was so tired she couldn't keep her eyes open a minute longer. When she dropped into bed, she always thought she would be able to do her homework in the morning, but by the time she'd fed the baby and rounded up some clothes that were mended and clean enough to wear to school, it was always too late.

Sherry knew that the school counselor was available to help people with problems, but she'd never known of anyone who asked the counselor for help with home problems. How could she get help? What should Sherry do?

Possible Discussion Topics:

1. Since we all have problems, how do we decide when to get help with them and when to try to solve them for ourselves?
2. Is getting homework done a school problem or a home problem?
3. What could the counselor do to help Sherry?

WHAT SHOULD CICELY DO?

Cicely has to cope with the problem of following in the footsteps of an older sister who always gave her teachers a lot of trouble.

It wasn't until third grade that Cicely felt that all the teachers were looking at her, expecting her to do the things her sister did. That kind of expecting wasn't good, because Jeanette had caused a lot a trouble at Eastern Elementary. She had been in fights, argued with the teachers, broken the glass in the side door and lied about it, made poor grades, and had been sent home countless times for misbehaving in class. The teachers were never glad to see

Jeanette in their classes. And now, Cicely felt sure that they dreaded seeing her, too.

It was especially bad this year with Mr. Wilcox. He and Jeanette hadn't gotten along at all, and he had sent her home more times than all the other teachers combined. Jeanette probably deserved it, Cicely knew. When Mr. Wilcox looked at Cicely on the first day of school, he said, "Are you Jeanette's sister?" And when she said "Yes," he placed her in the very first row right in front of his desk.

When the gym teacher asked the same question and got the same answer, it seemed to Cicely that he frowned.

In a way, Cicely couldn't blame them for being worried about her after having to put up with so much from Jeanette. But how could Cicely tell them that she and Jeanette were as different as cold and hot and that she had always liked school while Jeanette hated it?

How do you escape the shadow of a big sister or someone else in your family who has been in trouble? How do you make people like you for what you are, and not for what your family is? What should Cicely do?

Possible Discussion Topics:

1. Do you think most teachers would be willing to give Cicely a fair chance to prove what kind of a person she is?
2. May Cicely be imagining that some of the teachers are holding her sister's actions against her when they really aren't?
3. What might Cicely do to straighten things out between herself and her teachers?

WHAT SHOULD GLEN DO?

Glen discovers that the first group to befriend him at his new school is made up of rowdies. Now he wants to break away.

When Glen was going through the cafeteria line on his first day at Dale School, Jack Riley and his buddies started talking to him and invited him to eat lunch with them. They seemed to take it for granted from the start that

Glen would be a member of their gang.

Glen felt lucky to have made friends so soon at his new school. Before long, though, he decided that perhaps he had not been lucky at all. The kids in Jack's gang were loud and smart-alecky and acted bored with everything except seeing how many rules they could break and how many people they could bug.

They were in trouble half the time, and the teacher, Mrs. Hobart, didn't seem to realize that Glen didn't have anything to do with their acting up. She frowned at him as well as at the others in the gang.

Even worse, from Glen's point of view, Jack's crowd wouldn't give him a chance to make friends with other kids that he thought would be lots more fun to be with. There was George, for instance, who was interested in science and owned a good microscope. When he brought the microscope to school one day, Glen thought he saw his chance to get acquainted with him. He asked George if he could look through it, and George said sure, to come with him to his classroom. Just then one of the gang came by and yelled, "What are you sticking around with that creep for?" Glen was so ashamed he just walked away.

Glen was fascinated by how a boy named Paul could play the drums. One day he was watching Paul work the traps with his hands and feet—sort of like rubbing your stomach while you pat your head, Glen thought—and Jack came up and kicked the drum. "Clear out, you guys!" Paul growled. Glen realized then that the kids as well as Mrs. Hobart thought he was just like Jack and his crowd.

Glen wanted desperately to break away from the gang and make friends with kids like George and Paul, who enjoyed doing interesting things instead of horsing around, but he didn't know how to go about it.

What should Glen do?

Possible Discussion Topics:

1. Would Glen have been better off to have no friends for awhile rather than to have become buddies with Jack and his gang?
2. What could Glen do to show everybody that he doesn't want to belong to Jack's gang?
3. What can a class do to give a new pupil a chance to get to know everybody before deciding who he wants to pal around with?

WHAT SHOULD JACOB DO?

Jacob's been putting on an act since first grade—pretending to hate school and "sissy" things—thinking that's what he had to do to be "one of the boys."

When the teacher said that the class was going to start long division, everyone groaned. Jacob had wondered about dividing big numbers, so he thought long division might be interesting, but he groaned too, because the others did. When the bell for fire drill interrupted Miss Hibbing while she was reading a story aloud, the class cheered. Jacob wanted to hear the end of the story, but he cheered too, because the others did. When the principal asked all the classes to make safety posters and the gang said that was a sissy thing to do, Jacob chimed in, although he loved to make posters.

Ever since first grade, Jacob had been acting as though he disliked school, because most of the kids acted that way and he didn't want them to think he was an oddball. He wanted to be "one of the boys."

Jacob had them fooled so far, but this year he was afraid Miss Hibbing would give the show away. One day when he had made good grades on all his tests she had said, "I can't see why you don't like school when you do so well in your work."

"School's a big fat drag, that's all," Jacob had answered, and the kids had laughed.

In science one day Miss Hibbing gave everyone some beans to take home and plant. "Watch them grow," she said, "and when the leaves appear, bring the plants to school."

On the way home, most of the kids threw their beans away. Jacob, however, dropped his into his pocket, and when he got home he followed his teacher's instructions for planting the seeds in a tin can and put them in a sunny window.

In a few days the beans sprouted, and then some tiny leaves appeared. Before long the plants were growing so fast that he could almost see them getting bigger while he watched them. It all seemed like a miracle to Jacob, who'd never grown anything before. He was sure his plants were the best ever and he wanted very much for Miss Hibbing to see them. If he took them to school, though, he knew he would be laughed at. He dreaded that, but he was tired of having to cover up his real feelings.

What should Jacob do?

Possible Discussion Topics:
1. How can Jacob be himself, doing the things he likes to do, and still stay friends with the other kids?
2. Is it possible that some of the others might feel as Jacob does but might also be afraid to show it?
3. How is Jacob cheating himself?

WHAT SHOULD DAVID DO?

David likes odd-looking Mr. Crow and is delighted when he offers to substitute for his dad on Fathers' Night—until he thinks about what the kids will say.

David usually looked forward to talking with Mr. Crow on his way home from school. Today was different, though. He hoped that Mr. Crow would not be working in his garden, but there he was, waving his rake at David and smiling expectantly in his direction.

Walking toward him as slowly as he could, David took a long look at Mr. Crow and saw him as if he were a stranger rather than a good friend: The old man's clothes were wrinkled and dingy, his white hair straggled over his collar, and his glasses had been mended with a bit of string.

With a sinking feeling David admitted to himself that Mr. Crow did look a little like a tramp. Until a few days ago he'd never really thought about Mr. Crow's appearance except that he was usually smiling and that his face lit up with interest as he listened to whatever a person had to tell him.

David didn't know much about him except that he had been living in the neighborhood for many years, he could fix all kinds of broken toys, and he was wonderful to talk with. He would exclaim loudly over the good test papers that David showed him and was always curious to hear about what David was learning.

He was sympathetic too. For example, he had been almost as upset as David was to learn that Fathers' Night at school was on the same evening that David's dad was bowling in a tournament.

He had agreed that it wouldn't be so bad if David could take an uncle instead of his dad, but none of David's relatives lives within a hundred miles.

He had raked up leaves in thoughtful silence for several minutes and then his face had lighted up as he suggested, "Why don't I come to Fathers' Night? Of course I'm not a relative, but I couldn't feel prouder if I were—it would be a treat for me, too."

"Gee, thanks, Mr. Crow. That would be super," said David. He had meant it, too, until yesterday when he happened to tell Bunky Gaylord about the plan.

"Aw, you can't do that," said Bunky in disgust.

"Why not?" David wanted to know.

"Because he looks like an old tramp," said Bunky. "His name is supposed to be Mr. Crow, but I'll bet his name is really Mr. Scarecrow."

Ever since talking to Bunky, David had felt terribly mixed up. He couldn't decide what to do about Fathers' Night. He hated to be embarrassed, and Mr. Crow *did* look shabby and odd. Then too, his dad knew and liked Mr. Crow, but that didn't mean he'd approve of being replaced by him for the evening.

On the other hand, Mr. Crow was his most loyal friend, and it would hurt his feelings if David changed his mind about taking him to Fathers' Night.

"I sure wish I knew what to do," he muttered to himself as his dragging footsteps finally brought him to where Mr. Crow stood waiting for him. What should David do?

Possible Discussion Topics:

1. What values must David weigh in making his decision?
2. Is real friendship based on such things as looking like everyone else?
3. Do we sometimes have a *responsibility* to accept offers of help and kindness?

WHAT SHOULD KEVIN DO?

The deadline for Kevin to enter the art contest is tomorrow morning at nine-thirty but his dad comes home with tickets for a football game; they would have to leave at six-thirty.

Kevin turned and twisted on his bed. He wished he could forget about Mr. Dunlap. He wished that he had never heard of the art contest.

Kevin's problem was about a mobile—one of those things to hang from the ceiling. Kevin was unusually good at making them. He had been working on one based on the William Tell legend—a complicated one, loaded with red cardboard apples, wire bows, and little carved wooden arrows. Mr. Dunlap had suggested that Kevin finish it in time to enter it in the city-wide children's art contest at the public library.

Kevin had agreed. He had stayed after school every day for a week to put the finishing touches on the mobile. Usually Mr. Dunlap would be in the room, and while Kevin worked they would talk about how fine it would be if Kevin's entry won the first prize—a trip to the Los Angeles County Museum of History, Science, and Art for the student and his or her teacher.

When Kevin finished the mobile on Friday, Mr. Dunlap said, "You have real talent, Kevin. I have a hunch that this will win us the trip to Los Angeles. That would be as much of a treat for me as it would be for you. I haven't been to the museum in years. Remember the deadline for contest entries is nine-thirty tomorrow morning. You'd better take it down right after school."

Kevin was always waiting until the last minute to get things done. Instead of taking the mobile to the library as soon as school was out he took it home and went to John's house to try out his new racing bike. He planned to be at the library when it opened at nine o'clock the next morning to enter his exhibit.

When Kevin got home from John's house at dinner time, his father told him that he had been able to get hold of three tickets for a college football game being played in Los Angeles the next day. To get there in time for kick-off, they would have to leave at six-thirty in the morning.

Kevin had never seen college football except on TV. He hoped to be a college football player himself, someday. He was so excited that he never thought of the contest until he was ready for bed. Then he saw the mobile on his study table. If he left for Los Angeles at six-thirty, he couldn't enter the mobile.

Well, he thought, a football game was better than an art museum any day of the week. Who cared about the contest? *Oh, oh, Mr. Dunlap cared, that's who.* Mr. Dunlap was practically counting on Kevin's winning the contest. The trip to the museum meant a lot to him. What could Kevin say to him if the mobile wasn't even entered?

Perhaps he should just give up going to the game. But he wanted so much to go to a college game. Perhaps he could tell Mr. Dunlap that Butch, their new puppy, had chewed up the mobile.

What should Kevin do?

Possible Discussion Topics:

1. What is Kevin's responsibility to Mr. Dunlap?
2. Does Kevin have a responsibility to himself and the artwork he created for the contest?
3. In the long-run, which will be more meaningful to Kevin—the football game or entering, and possibly winning, the art contest.

WHAT SHOULD MARLENE DO?

Once seemed not too bad, but now Marlene's friends are making a habit of shoplifting.

Instead of going straight home after the first day of school, Marlene and three of her fourth-grade friends stopped at the shopping center to buy their school supplies. They picked out the pencils, pads, and erasers they needed and were about to take them to the checkout desk when Julie, who was new, said, "Let's see if we can snitch something. That's what we used to do at my old school. It's loads of fun." She led the way to another aisle, picked up a green plastic purse, and put it under her coat.

"Now all of you walk close to me so the bulge won't show," she said.

Talking loudly, the others crowded around her and they walked out of the store. Once outside, they laughed until the tears came.

"Well, that was pretty scary," Marlene said. "Now we'd better toss it back inside the store and run."

"We can't do that," Julie said. "The floor manager might call the police or our folks."

The police? Parents? Marlene felt sick. That night she couldn't get to sleep because she kept thinking of what might have happened if they'd been caught. Apparently the other kids didn't feel as she did, however, and only a couple of days later, when Carol said that she wanted to stop at the store and buy a birthday present for her, Pat and Julie said they would go into the store with her. "We'll do some shopping, too," Julie said, giggling.

"I have to go on home," Marlene said. "I have my ballet lesson."

"You missed some real fun," her friends told her the next morning. They showed her a lipstick and a box of eye makeup they had taken.

"You don't use makeup. What do you want with that stuff?" Marlene asked.

"Don't be a drag," Julie said. "We had the fun of sneaking the things out of the store, and next time we might be able to get some things we really want."

The friends sounded as though they were going to make a regular thing of seeing what they could steal. Marlene wondered if she should tell their parents or their teacher. If they kept up their shoplifting sooner or later they'd get caught and that might mean they'd be arrested. Marlene was afraid, though, that if she told on the others, they'd tell her parents that she had been along when Julie took the purse.

What should Marlene do?

Possible Discussion Topics:

1. Since Marlene was involved in only one stealing incident, does she have any responsibility to tell?
2. Is Marlene any less guilty than the others if she does nothing to stop the thefts?
3. How does shoplifting hurt all of a store's customers?

WHAT SHOULD IRENE DO?

Irene feels lost and lonely because her parents have separated; now she realizes that her school work is suffering, also.

For quite some time Irene had realized that something wasn't right between her mother and father. Frequently her dad didn't get home in time for supper, and sometimes she had been in bed a long time when she heard his footstep on the stairs. She worried about this and about the angry voices she heard sometimes coming from her parents' bedroom.

Still, once she got to school where her friends were, she was able to push her unhappy thoughts to the back of her mind. She had a lot of fun with the other kids—spending the night at the home of her best friend on weekends, baking cookies, or playing boxball after school.

Then Irene's parents told her they weren't going to live together any longer, and her father moved to another town. Everything changed. At home, Irene felt alone and lost. Her mother was usually there, but she was different. Her eyes were red and swollen all the time, and no matter what Irene tried to talk to her about, she never seemed interested. Her father did come to take her for a ride or to the movies every other Sunday, but it seemed to Irene that just as she got ready to talk to him about what was bothering her, it was time for him to leave.

Irene's lost and lonely feelings carried over to school. Things seemed as changed at school as they were at home. It seemed to her that her friends weren't as nice as they used to be and that the teacher ignored her. She started to do poorly in her school work, because in the midst of studying, she'd start to think about how miserable she felt.

Why had her father left her? Had she done something bad to make him want to leave her and mother? Why were her friends and the teacher so mean to her just when she felt sick inside and needed them the most? She didn't know where to turn for help. What should Irene do?

Possible Discussion Topics:

1. What makes Irene feel everyone at school owes her special attention?
2. Is Irene at fault because her parents have separated?
3. Does it help to talk about unhappy feelings with someone else? Who might Irene talk to about her problems?